Within Thy Silence

Words for The Prayer of Stillness

First published by O Books, 2010
O Books is an imprint of John Hunt Publishing Ltd., The Bothy, Deershot Lodge, Park Lane, Ropley,
Hants, SO24 0BE, UK
office1@o-books.net
www.o-books.net

Distribution in:	South Africa
	Stephan Phillips (pty) Ltd
UK and Europe	Email: orders@stephanphillips.com
Orca Book Services	Tel: 27 21 4489839 Telefax: 27 21 4479879
orders@orcabookservices.co.uk	
Tel: 01202 665432 Fax: 01202 666219	Text copyright The Fellowship of Contemplative
Int. code (44)	Prayer 2008
USA and Canada	Design: Stuart Davies
NBN	ISBN: 978 1 84694 266 2
custserv@nbnbooks.com	
Tel: 1 800 462 6420 Fax: 1 800 338 4550	All rights reserved. Except for brief quotations
	in critical articles or reviews, no part of this
Australia and New Zealand	book may be reproduced in any manner without
Brumby Books	prior written permission from the publishers.
sales@brumbybooks.com.au	
Tel: 61 3 9761 5535 Fax: 61 3 9761 7095	The rights of The Fellowship of Contemplative
	Prayer as author have been asserted in
Far East (offices in Singapore, Thailand,	accordance with the Copyright, Designs and
Hong Kong, Taiwan)	Patents Act 1988.
Pansing Distribution Pte Ltd	
kemal@pansing.com	A CIP catalogue record for this book is available
Tel: 65 6319 9939 Fax: 65 6462 5761	from the British Library.

Printed by Digital Book Print

O Books operates a distinctive and ethical publishing philosophy in
all areas of its business, from its global network of authors to
production and worldwide distribution.

Within Thy Silence

Words for The Prayer of Stillness

The commentaries in this book
were written by members of
The Fellowship of Contemplative Prayer
Compiled and edited
by

Martin Tunnicliffe

BOOKS

Winchester, UK
Washington, USA

CONTENTS

* * *

Abbreviations

AV	Authorised Version (King James Bible)
GNB	Good News Bible (Today's English Version)
JB	Jerusalem Bible
NEB	New English Bible
NIV	New International Version
NRSV	New Revised Standard Version
REB	Revised English Bible
RSV	Revised Standard Version
RV	Revised Version 1881-85
TEV	Today's English Version (Good News Bible)

Jesus said: My Words are Spirit and Life
John 6.63

Foreword

by the Bishop of Birmingham

As the world and even the church changes all around us, accepting the challenge to go deeper in prayer, nurturing our relationship with God, through Jesus Christ in the power of the Holy Spirit is instrumental in our being transformed into the likeness of Jesus.

In this nourishing book, the Fellowship of Contemplative Prayer provides us with a practical and attractive companion to entering into the stillness of the presence of God. The book is edited by Martin Tunnicliffe whose long and distinguished parochial ministry in the Diocese of Birmingham has ensured that this book has an accessibility and simplicity that will be of great help and comfort to those who consider themselves to be either beginners or challenged in their prayer life.

The book is also earthed in scripture. There are some wonderful insights into biblical teaching as well as a helpful way of using the Bible in prayer.

I very much hope that this book becomes a wise and generous companion in prayer.

I trust, also, that it will help you to reflect upon your own pattern of prayer in seeking God's grace in renewing and strengthening your journey with Him. This will not be a solitary process, but, as outlined in the book, strengthened by conversation and practice within your households, with colleagues and in your church fellowship.

The Rt Revd David Urquhart
Bishop of Birmingham

Preface

Our Lady of Advent

Lowly handmaid of the Lord,
Love awakened by His grace,
God chooseth thee.
In joy accepteth thou the angel's news
From the Lord of Life.

Good ground enriched by God's own breath,
Thy mortal clay the seed doth nourish;
Blessed art thou.
Within thy silence groweth the Word,
Thy burden, Jesus Christ.

Mother alert to all hearts' joys
Thou prayest, and at festal time
God's sign is manifest.
Now comes the hour when God revealeth
The glory of His Son.

Thou joy of the Church throughout all ages,
Thou bearest our hope of heaven's realm;
The living Christ!
Thou Star of Advent, enlighten our path
To the eternal dawn.

Anon.

This delicate poem includes the title of this book and also in a sense encapsulates its contents. The essence of the prayer of stillness and silence, contemplative prayer, is to allow the living Word of God to grow within you. This is a sharing in the mystery of Incarnation, the Word-made-flesh, and as such is analogous to the role of Mary, the Mother of the Lord, *theotokos*, God-bearer. As we sing at Christmas time, "Be born in us today."

The Sayings in this book are all aspects of the living Word of God and therefore aspects of Christ. They have already been a focus of contemplative attention over many years among a number of people drawn to the prayer of silence. My task has been to select the Sayings, to provide a few commentaries, and to edit commentaries written by other people. Much of the material has therefore been contributed anonymously by fellow-members of The Fellowship of Contemplative Prayer, and I want to record my gratitude to them for having made their contributions available.

I am also indebted to the Bishop of Birmingham, the Rt Revd David Urquhart for taking time in a very busy schedule to write the Foreword, and to the publisher John Hunt for encouragement and valuable guidance. The book is dedicated to the glory of God who, in the Word-made-flesh, shows us with clarity the way to salvation.

Martin Tunnicliffe
Solihull 2009

Start Now . . .

The important words in this book are the ones in bold print at the head of each page from page ten onwards. For this is a practical handbook, not a treatise about prayer. What I am saying now is no more than an introductory 'patter,' a few brief comments to set the scene for you. The sooner you get on with *doing*, or at least trying to do the prayer of stillness the better. But in the context of today's world, engagement in serious prayer, especially of the silent and contemplative kind, is so counter-cultural as to be almost subversive. So some brief introductory remarks will be helpful.

The world is a noisier place than it has ever been. A media-driven culture seems designed to prevent people from being or becoming reflective, quiet, non-active and still. Waking hours, even leisure hours, are usually filled with activity. And when people finally sit still they mostly prefer to be watching a flickering screen to distract them from a growing dread of inner emptiness and the apparent futility of a society and probably a whole civilization that seems to be sadly off-course.

Christianity should be a means of steering the world on course. This is a role that the Church has played with greatly varying degrees of competence down the ages. It is, however, important to realise that, traditionally, the Church has striven to play this part by paying close attention to the Word of God by means of reflection, meditation and contemplative prayer. To look at the list of *activities* of the average 'successful' Church of today it becomes clear how the Church itself has been infected by the prevailing culture and forgotten this part of its tradition.

If it should be thought that to engage in the prayer of stillness and silence is to be dodging the Church's responsibility for social involvement and action for justice and on behalf of the poor, then I call on a powerful witness to put the other point of view.

Kenneth Leech is a leading writer on the Church's social responsibility and also on spirituality. A great deal of his ministry has been spent in London's vibrant and often turbulent East End, also among the providers and clientele of night-life entertainment in the district of Soho. In his book *The Eye of the Storm* [*] he writes:

I have come to see, as an activist, the central place of silence in my life and in the lives of all who would work for peace and justice at a more than surface level. There is a sense in which silent waiting on God is the heart of prayer, a simple abiding in emptiness, weakness and attention, a recognition of the fact that it is the Spirit who prays within us in inarticulate groanings (Romans 8.26)...

The hyperactive person, whether community worker or pastor, who has not given time for inner stillness will soon communicate to others nothing more than his or her inner tiredness and exhaustion of spirit — not a very kind thing to do to people who have enough problems of their own.

Silence is an integral part of ministry and of effective Christian action. In silence we open ourselves up to the activity of God and to the movements of history. If it is important to listen to the voice of God, to try to discern and distinguish the voice of God amidst the conflicting voices around and within us, it is also important to listen to the voices of the world, particularly the hidden, neglected voices. It is important to listen carefully to the language of silence, the silence of crushed, broken, battered people. A contemplative, reflective approach is a necessary part of any sustained social action, and without that base it is bound to become superficial and to lack both depth and staying power. Silence helps to create stillness and the ability to hear. It also creates a climate of discernment and scrutiny, of persistent interrogation, of

*Darton, Longman & Todd 1992

inner struggle to discern the signs...

Linked with the silence is the prayerful and meditative use of the Bible...I find myself more and more needing to stress both the place of Scripture in the life of prayer and action, and the importance of a biblical spirituality.

This is very important teaching for Christians in any age, but most particularly in these turbulent and often puzzling and fearful times. In fact they are relevant for followers of any authentic religious tradition. This book is primarily for Christians but members of other religions will find a similar vein of teaching in their sacred texts and among their more enlightened theologians and thinkers.

So — start now! I stress that this is a practical, not a theoretical book. It is the sort of book whose pages should become dog-eared and loose like those of the best Bibles. In fact, if you use this book as I suggest you do, your Bible should suffer a bit as well. Because, as I said earlier, the most important words are God's Words at the head of each page. To be more precise in the language of the Spirit, these are the Word of God. Any other words you may come across, including those you are now reading, are subordinate and incidental. They are human speech, written to help you listen more attentively to what God is saying. My hope is that eventually these lesser words, having done their job, will fall away and that the Word which God speaks will, at least for certain periods of time, become the sole focus of your attention.

In order for this to happen, you will need to take some time out, a few moments when you can be quiet on your own. You won't need any equipment apart from this book and a chair to sit on. Nor will you require any special skill or knowledge. Let's say, then, that you've got 15 or 20 minutes when you can be alone in a quiet place.

Now try this:

Sit on your chair, upright but relaxed. If you have some physical disability, then just be as relaxed as you can in whatever position is easiest. Sit still for a few moments. Try to let your worries subside. Take a few deep breaths, then control your breathing so that you breathe a little more deeply, in and out, but without any strain.

Now, open this book at random.
Look at the Saying printed at the top of the page.
It may convey some thought or idea to you straight away.
Or it may not.
No matter either way.
Read the commentary.
Look at the Saying again and make sure you know it by heart.
Now, put the book down.

This shouldn't take you more than three or four minutes.

All you need do now, sitting quietly and relaxed, is gently to repeat the Saying over and over again in your mind for the rest of the time you have available. Forget the commentary; forget your own thoughts; ignore any noises off. Just be alive to the Saying; let it sink in, and realise that God is speaking those words to you.

This is 'God Direct.'

As the time draws to a close, just say, "Thank you, Lord, for the gift of your Word." Then go about your daily business. Later in the day, if you have more time (or tomorrow if you haven't) you might want to repeat this prayer-exercise. But use the same Saying for two or three days, perhaps every day for a week, before you move on to another one.

After a week or two praying in this way, you should know if God is nudging you into this kind of contemplative prayer, or whether you are not ready for it at this stage in your life. If the latter, then I suggest you put the book away for a bit, and try again in a few weeks, or perhaps a few months, time. If on the other hand you feel drawn to continue, then you are beginning a journey of exploration. In that case, read the Postscript at the end of this book where I say a bit more about it and suggest what you should do next.

May God be with you along the way.

A to Z

"I AM the beginning and the ending, the Almighty"
(Revelation 1.8)

This is a declaration that Saint John, when he heard it trumpeted from heaven inside his cave on the island of Patmos, could not ignore. First and foremost, the heavenly words put him in direct touch with the historic nation of Israel who, like John, were given this Saying when they were in exile. God's people were at a very low ebb, in a place and at a point, it seemed, of no return. John would have felt much the same on Patmos island, cut off from the Christian communities he knew and loved, among whom he had been a respected leader.

Those communities, like faith communities today, were a mixed bunch with many ups and downs: and some of them shared with John the sense of God-forsaken-ness. They, too, were at a low ebb, and vulnerable in a hostile world of paganism, strange gods and unfriendly powers.

To them, through John, and to us also through him, God speaks the solemn reminder: I AM the beginning and the ending — the A to Z of all that is. In Isaiah 41 verse 4, following this revelation of God's word of power, the exiled prophet is inspired to pour scorn on the futility of all human pretensions at power, and on the silly alternative gods that people construct for themselves.

Alright — the battle is joined between good and evil: alright — people are going to get hurt and the faithful must endure suffering. That is what we read about in the turbulent book of Revelation. But like the prophet before him, John glimpses the future triumph of God's legions of angels, the victory of truth and justice, and the vindication of God's people. There can be no gainsaying the almightiness of God who is sovereign of *all* creation, not just part of it.

'A' and 'O' are the first and last letters of the Greek alphabet. John, as fluent in Hebrew as in Greek, knew that 'Aleph' and 'Tau,' the first and last letters of the Hebrew alphabet, represent *all* the letters in between. This Saying reminds us that God is not just in the distant past and ultimate future. He is the eternal present — the I AM, God-with-us on the side of goodness, beauty and truth against all evil, ugliness and falsity.

A Loaf for Life

"I AM the bread of life"
(John 6.35)

The context for this Word, for which there are no other parallels in the Gospels, is the early part of John, chapter six, where John is describing the feeding of the five thousand. Afterwards, when Jesus journeys to the other side of lake Gennesaret, the crowd come to try and find him. And Jesus knows why: "You are looking for me because you ate the bread and had all you wanted." The crowd want another free meal. They ask for bread twice more during this chapter and begin to moan and grumble when they do not get it. There is criticism, argument, and many of them leave.

This is a total misunderstanding of the nature of the 'bread' which God is offering his people, and us, through this food. The bread being offered is spiritual sustenance, daily strengthening.

It is tempting and attractive to listen to the crowds following Jesus and think rather disparagingly of them. Yet the same motives and misunderstandings may also be in us. The offer of bread focuses us on our desires. What do we want? Perhaps our deepest desire is for something concrete: a better job, income, or marriage. Or perhaps we search for an experience: popularity, excitement, or power.

What does Christ say to these hopes? He says the same as to the crowd: "I AM the Bread of Life." God has sent Jesus to initiate relationship, to live intimately with us. This is good, but it often does not seem or feel to be what we need or want. Perhaps we are tempted to turn away in frustration or anger. This Word encourages us, however, to express these emotions and offer them to God in their rawness. Our pleading can learn to be content with "I AM the Bread of Life." A food which sustains us and which is to live by.

This Word recalls us to the reality that, to become food, bread has to be broken, and shared. This is what we do through our prayer for others: for the hungry, the disappointed, those tempted to give up, those who need sustenance, those who administer aid to the deprived, and those who minister in God's name to the spiritually hungry.

Action Stations

"Go and see . . . go and do"
(Mark 6.38 and Luke 10.37)

Here are two Dominical commands, each in their way as compelling as any of the Ten Commandments. The first is to the disciples of Jesus, appalled at the prospect of feeding hungry crowds in a remote place. The second is to the lawyer who asked the famous, perhaps infamous, question, "Who is my neighbour?" The second command follows very naturally on the first, for when you "go and see," i.e. when you become aware of God's goodness and love in creation and salvation, the more you are moved to "go and do" in terms of making the good news known by word and deed.

The miracle of feeding is required as much for crowds who are hungry for the Word of God as it is for the filling of empty bellies. Jesus asked about resources, "What is already there?" and followed this with the order, "Go and see." "Go and see" tells us not to accept blindly what we are told about lack of resources. We are conditioned to believe that people suffer because there is not enough to go round. The fact is that human misery and deprivation are man-made tragedies. Most of those who suffer today do so as a result of the greed and selfishness of other people; and the small proportion of the human race whose poor circumstances are truly the result of natural disaster could be readily relieved if their more fortunate neighbours (including ourselves) were truly unselfish. Those who have a spiritual vision will discern God's superabundant provision of grace and love *and* resources, however much these good things may be masked by the sinfulness of humankind bent on wilful self-satisfaction.

The more people open their eyes to see God at work and their ears to hear his Word, the greater will be the chances for the hungry to be fed, both physically and spiritually.

In other words, as we continually re-sensitise ourselves to the key question, "Who is my neighbour?" so humanity will see the good sense in obeying the command that requires us to emulate the Good Samaritan, "Go and do thou likewise."

All Change

"Do not be afraid: from now on you will be . . ."
(Luke 5.10)

You will probably want to complete this Saying; and you no doubt know that it ends "fishers of men." But I have left it unfinished on purpose. The context is the calling by Jesus of his first followers. Jesus teaches from his floating pulpit, re-interpreting the nature of God's Kingdom and then tests the nature of the disciples. Surviving clay tablets record some trade figures about the fishing in the lake and show that the fish for export were dried and, in Rome itself, were considered a delicacy. To assume that Peter and his friends were simple poor fishermen is too naive; they clearly enjoyed a freedom of movement and independence and some flexibility in their working hours.

After teaching the crowds, Jesus commands the fishermen to go on another trip knowing that they will be reluctant after a hard day's fruitless night. Peter agrees with some protest and they are overwhelmed with fish. This amazing catch is a sign and an occasion for Jesus to call on their help for rather more than they were prepared, especially as it led to a complete change of work. That's how it is for some people.

I had such an experience, though ordered slightly differently. While I was a salesman, I was called to work in the Church's ministry. There were two outcomes. First, I was greatly afraid: and second, I suddenly began to sell much more effectively. I was afraid when I considered the task ahead, afraid of the change in lifestyle, afraid that I was not good enough. My miraculous "catch of fish" in more successful selling I cannot account for at all, any more than the disciples could account for theirs.

This Saying, with the end chopped off, speaks eloquently and with great relevance to anyone who is on the point of a great change of direction. It could be a job change, or a promotion to a post of greater responsibility: it could be the prospect of marriage or the arrival of a new baby. You could no doubt think of a great number of other possibilities of a radical change of direction. Our prayerful relationship with God can help to settle our anxieties. And the phrase "from now on you will be," even in its unfinished state, contains the positive assurance that *you will be* under the guiding hand of God, come what may.

Amazing Grace

"I came to call sinners"
(Matthew 9.13 JB)

On first approach this sounds and feels like a slightly forbidding and off-putting Word to use for contemplation, but actually it can be experienced as liberating. The Saying comes immediately following the call of Matthew to become a disciple, and occurs in his house where Jesus goes as a guest. As with the other early disciples, no mention is made of why Matthew followed Jesus, but what is clear, and related to our contemplative word, is that Matthew is regarded as unclean. He was a social outcast. Tax collectors were collaborators with the Roman imperial authorities, were considered to be disloyal, and were suspected of treason. In addition, they made their margin of profit through extortion of more than was legally due, and were viewed as exploitative. Roman money itself was unclean, and so was someone who touched it.

Often the word 'sinner' was used as a technical term for members of despised trades like Matthew. The calling of a tax collector into the company of the disciples of Jesus was, for all these reasons, a sign that the Kingdom would be given to those who had put themselves outside the religious and ceremonial law. The Kingdom is given to those who have no righteousness of their own. The grace of God is primary.

By inviting sinners to share meals with him Jesus is revealing the generosity of God. It is true probably that many Christian people expect and ask too much of themselves, an attainment of a certain standard or set of achievements. A lot of our activity may be fuelled by guilt. It is a discouraging and exhausting business. This is why this Word for contemplation is so liberating, because it reminds us that we are not accepted, called or commissioned by God because of what we have done or achieved. We are called and accepted for what we know ourselves to be . . . as sinners. As fallible people who often choose the wrong path. This is all right because we are called and accepted by God's grace.

In intercession we may choose to use this Saying to pray for those whom we find socially unclean or religiously uncomfortable, those whom we regard as not 'one of us'.

And God Said

"My Word ... shall prosper in the thing whereto I send it"
(Isaiah 55.11 RV)

One day a man found that he was losing the use of his legs. His son persuaded him to go to hospital for examination. There was found to be a spinal obstruction. The son was about to start on a holiday in the Far East. He wanted to cancel it. The hospital said that if the father came through the first days after the operation, all would be well. The son waited. The operation was successful, so he went on holiday as planned.

Two weeks later, 6000 miles from home, a sudden wave of depression swept over him. He could not account for it. A man he was talking to noticed his distress and was told about the father's illness. The man turned out to be a missionary. He said, "We have a prayer meeting this evening; please come, and we will pray for your father."

Back home, the hospital was worried. The patient had been going downhill. Then quite suddenly, the tide turned. The patient began to recover. Checking up later, father and son found that the change began on the very day and at the very hour of those prayers on the other side of the world. Many of us will have known of such cases of healing, almost replicas of that of the nobleman's son recorded by Saint John (4.50).

Why has the Word of the Lord such power, spoken in any language used in any location? Because his Word is the mentally or verbally *uttered sign* of his absolute power. Rather as the seal on a legal document is a sign of its binding authority.

God assures us that if we faithfully offer ourselves in intercession to be channels for his Word to go out to others, we can be certain that the Word will reach the one to whom it is sent, through our intercession. Even more, it will do in that one whatever God has planned, whether we think it best for him or not. We are not always the best judge of what a person needs; but God knows precisely, and in his good time he will meet that need.

Angels of the Lord

"Go and use this strength of yours . . . it is I who send you"
(Judges 6.14 REB)

Each year in September the Church loves to celebrate the Feast of the Angels*. Scripture knows little of the decorative angels of popular art and modern Nativity plays. If wings are mentioned, this is because flight was a mysterious attribute denied to human beings. Halos are symbolic of the divine aura of spiritual light, the "glory of the Lord". Angels in the Bible appear in human guise, but as temporary visitors of great power and authority. They tend to strike fear into those whom they visit (Isaiah 6.5; Daniel 8.17; Luke 2.9). Because they are God's messengers, their words are equivalent to Divine utterance.

This month's Saying was spoken by God's messenger to Gideon. The words came as a total surprise. Gideon was about his daily chores. He had no pretensions to be a leader. When he hears God's command to become the deliverer of his people, his response is candid: "How can I save Israel? Look at my clan: it is the weakest, and I am the least in my father's family." But Gideon is roundly told to get up and go, in the strength that God has supplied, using abilities that he never realised he had.

This pattern of the seemingly weak made powerful for good by the grace of God comes so frequently in the Bible that we do well to pay close attention to it. Consider the child Samuel (1 Samuel 3. 4), the shepherd-boy David (1 Samuel 16.11), the reluctant prophet Jeremiah (Jeremiah 1.6), even Saint Paul (2 Corinthians 12.9) – and supremely, of course, the Mother of the Lord who, following her angelic visitation became our constant

* 29 September

reminder that God "has exalted the humble and meek" (Luke 1.52).

To receive this Saying will challenge us to reconsider our vocation as children of God, possessing gifts of which we may as yet be totally unaware, and empowered by God to play some significant part in the fulfilling of his purposes, even if we are not yet certain what this might entail. And in intercession, this Word will help to bring new strength and openings for service even to those who appear at present to be beset with problems.

At Home

"Make your home in me, as I make mine in you"
(John 15.4 JB)

This Saying comes from the John's 15th chapter. You will be familiar with it in the form "Abide in me (or 'dwell in me') as I in you". This time we'll make use of an alternative translation.

Jesus is speaking to his disciples shortly before his death. He is trying to prepare them for the time when he will leave them, when they must live without his physical presence. He speaks of himself as the vine, and his followers as branches of the vine, and he says "Make your home in me, as I make mine in you."

The home is, or should be, a place of safety, of security. It is the place where we are cared for and nurtured, and where we grow. It is the place where we can be ourselves. We may go out to work and we return home for rest and refreshment. Home is a place of hospitality, into which we can invite our friends, or people in need.

Some of us have recently moved house, or are about to move. It is very unsettling. It seems to chip away at our security. Change makes us feel uncomfortable. Perhaps this is especially true for women, for whom the home seems to be an extension of their personality.

But change is an inevitable part of life. We need to find security in the midst of change. Saint Paul managed it. He said "I have learned, in whatsoever state I am, therewith to be content" (Philippians 4.11).

Etty Hillesum, a Dutch Jewess who was displaced from her home during the war, and finally died in Auschwitz, wrote, "We must be our own country." Security is not to be found in material things. We must look elsewhere. Jesus invites us to find our security in him, so that when change comes, whether welcome or unwelcome, it doesn't disturb the core of our being.

At the centre of Christian worship is a sacramental meal when worshippers receive in faith the life of Jesus, body and blood. No clearer sign than this could be given to the friends of Christ that he would make his home in the hearts of the faithful.

Bang Bang

**"My Word is like fire and like a hammer
which breaks a rock in pieces"**
(Jeremiah 23.29 NRSV)

In this Saying, God is speaking to us through the prophet Jeremiah. There is a built-in ambiguity. Fire can cleanse and purify; it can also be terrifyingly destructive like a house fire. On the other hand, in the process of refining, you need the destructive power of fire to sort out the pure metal from the dross (Malachi 3.2-3). A hammer can also be destructive; but of course it is used constructively and creatively in quarrying, carpentry, geology and toffee-breaking! From a block of stone Michelangelo carved statuary in which austerity and classic beauty were powerfully harmonised. He had to chip and hammer away in order to create. God needs to chip and hammer away at us, to shape or reshape us, to help our personal and spiritual development. As the sculptor knows the potential within the rock, so God knows our potential. The sculptor works from the outside, God from within.

This Saying also emphasises our dependence on God for our inward growth. If we are faithful in our contemplation of this Word, facing the bits of ourselves we do not like, repeating and receiving God's statement about the power of his Word, it will slowly but surely sink below the surface of our human nature to transform us from the inside out. His Word which is spirit and life will bit by bit change us towards the Self he created and intended us to become.

The prophet Ezekiel heard the Lord saying to his people: "None of my words will be delayed … the Word which I speak will be performed" (Ezekiel 12.28). His fellow prophet in exile shared the same conviction (Isaiah 55.11). God works on us gradually and patiently, like a master craftsman. As we get into the habit of silent listening to these words from the Divine Source, letting them as it were be prayed within us, we shall begin to see things from God's perspective. In our daily lives, in our relationships, and even in the unpleasant and painful things that are bound to happen to us sooner or later, we shall be able to retain the inner conviction that God is truly at work in us, as he is in all creation.

Be Quiet

"In stillness and in staying quiet, there lies your strength"
(Isaiah 30.15 NEB)

God spoke these words to Isaiah at a time of political and social turmoil with the command that the prophet should pronounce them to the people. The present age is a time of unrest and noise. This is largely because, like the people of God in Isaiah's day, our people are looking elsewhere than God-ward for salvation. Consequently, they will never find what they seek — calm in life's storms and ultimate satisfaction for their deep (yet hardly recognised) spiritual longings; because these blessings are to be found only in the Lord I AM who is the source of them. That is why we cultivate the art of listening, deep listening, to His Word. In his lovely book *Anam Cara* (Soul Friend) John O'Donohue writes:

> There is a very important distinction to be made between listening and hearing. Sometimes we listen to things, but we never hear them. True listening brings us in touch even with that which is unsaid and unsayable. Sometimes the most important thresholds of mystery are places of silence. To be genuinely spiritual is to have great respect for the possibilities and presence of silence. Martin Heidegger says that true listening is worship. When you listen with your soul, you come into rhythm and unity with the music of the universe. Through friendship and love, you learn to attune your self to the silence, to the thresholds of mystery where your life enters the life of your beloved and their life enters yours.

This applies equally whether 'the beloved' is human or divine. The love between human beings is, at its best, closely bound up with what Bishop Stephen Verney called "the dance of love" within God the Trinity and between God, his creation, and human beings. Joyce Huggett writes:

> Silence is the context in which God most readily reveals himself, in which his voice is most clearly heard and where he rains on us the riches of his love. Silence is the language of lovers. It is therefore the language God delights to use to woo us to himself and the vocabulary we choose to express our response to his love. Silence before God has little to do with achieving, but a great deal to do with receiving.
> (*Open to God*)

Being and Giving

"I AM the bread of life: I will give"
(John 6. 48-51)

Check out Exodus 3.14. This is why I AM is in capital letters, for it is the sacred Name of God revealed to Moses. Four letters in Hebrew; three in English: utterly mysterious, yet containing in themselves all that ever was, is, or could be expressed. Eternally in the present tense, outside the limits of time, before the beginning began, and after the ending has ended. I AM; complete being and cause, sustainer and ultimate goal of all that was, is, or ever could be.

This is God's self-description. There are other disclosures, but they are all glimpses of the same basic statement from different perspectives, like a jewel perpetually turning before our eyes to reveal ever more of its facets. Infinite in variety, so no mind can comprehend I AM, yet with basic and fundamental integrity. Before all doing, there must be being. Our age aspires to doing mighty things, but all these are fruitless unless we progress in being in accordance with the will of God. For human *beings* derive their *being* from The Being, the I AM. Therefore "seek first of all the kingdom of God" because "without me (the I AM) you can do nothing." (Matthew 6.33; John 15.5)

In John's Gospel particularly, Jesus accrues this Divine Name to himself, not for self-glorification, but to express truths about the nature of God relating to humankind. In this Saying there is no vague statement of future policy, but an expression of God's eternal will; utterly simple, eternally wonderful. The ultimate Being will be the ultimate giver, even to total self-giving.

In this respect the attitude of the world is in conflict with the revealed Word of God. For the world believes that in order to live you must acquire and retain. But the Word says, in order to live (i.e. really to be alive from this moment on and in eternity) you must give. The seal on this truth is set by the Word-become-Flesh himself, who was raised to life after, and because of, his uttermost giving of him-self. In God, the I AM, living and giving are the same. The living proof of this is seen in the life, death, resurrection, and glorification of Jesus Christ.

Belonging

"I am the Good Shepherd"
(John 10. 14)

The image of a shepherd and his sheep referring to clergy and their congregations seems inappropriate in today's urban culture. And lay people in churches are not usually very pleased to be referred to as "sheep". Yet the pastoral vocabulary lingers on, and pastoral care is still widely understood to denote a warm and creative relationship between a helper and someone in need, whether in churches or in other sections of society. So the words 'shepherd,' 'pastoral' and 'flock' still carry a strong sense of caring, even to the modern mind. For we all need to feel that we belong somewhere, and to someone, not in the sense of being taken over and made to feel inferior, but in the sense of being in relationship and being valued.

When Jesus spoke these words, they were for his hearers a homely and familiar metaphor. But they were something more. In the first instance, the words 'I am.' *ego eimi* in the Greek text, denote the sacred Name of God. Jesus uses it in other contexts in John's Gospel, much to the annoyance of the representatives of the established religion who considered that he was blaspheming. But the common people saw Jesus as a God person and they could accept and appreciate the metaphor, because Jesus clearly demonstrated in himself the loving-kindness of God.

In addition, the words were to some extent subversive. The word 'Shepherd' was a familiar Old Testament word used for the political leaders. The prophets, particularly the prophet Ezekiel, had lodged a strong critique against the 'bad shepherds' of their time, leaders who did not particularly care for anyone except themselves and their own status. Under bad leadership, the people, in particular the poor and vulnerable people in society, will suffer disproportionately through no fault of their own. There is a very similar Word from God in Ezekiel 34.15: "I myself will be the shepherd of my flock."

It is comforting to hear this Saying when we are feeling unwanted or let down. It is also useful to remember it when, in accordance with the instruction from St Paul (1 Timothy 2.1-2), we pray for those in positions of responsibility and those who have to endure bad leadership.

Best Possession

"I will walk among you . . . ye shall be MY people"
(Leviticus 26.12 AV)

It is a daunting thought that the whole of the Bible is written within the context of the institution of slavery. Yet within that context, when it was possible for one human being to be quite literally the *possession* of another, great spiritual truths came to light. One of these was the idea of people being and becoming *God's* possession.

I suppose that slavery in its most benign aspect meant that owners were morally responsible for the slaves and deeply aware of them as human beings, with an obligation for their total well-being as if they were members of their own family. In this sense, then, arises the image of God being in an absolutely benign possessive relationship with human beings who are themselves totally reliant on him — MY people.

This image becomes more urgently powerful in the writings of the prophet of the exile (Isaiah 40-55, see especially chapter 43). This was a time when the people of faith felt lost and God-forsaken. They (and we sometimes) needed to be forcefully reminded that human beings, in particular those who are of "the household of faith", are still God's possession. "I have called thee by name, thou art MINE" (43.1). It used to irritate me as a child when grown-ups who couldn't be bothered to ask me my name used to call me 'sonny Jim': even more as an adult when they called me 'Jack.' I felt instinctively that they didn't care much about me.

Christians, especially at Christmas time, rejoice in the Biblical truths that God is very much 'with us' (the meaning of *Emmanuel*) and that he cares enough to know our names. The promise is stated in Leviticus "I will walk among you." That made the God of Israel a very different being, and infinitely more interesting, than the gods of Babylon which could only move if they were dragged around on trolleys. And as we know, the promise was dramatically fulfilled in the human birth of Christ in Jesus of Nazareth, and in the holy life which followed this quietly stunning event. The One whose dear possession we are, went about among us to draw us even more closely to Himself.

Big Question

"What doest thou here?"
(1 Kings 19. 9 & 13 AV)

The question from the Lord I AM to Elijah is more powerful than the violence of the stormy wind and earthquake that preceded it. Read and ponder the whole of 1 Kings chapter 19. If any scripture was "written for our learning," this is a prime example. The encounter between Elijah and God is as seminal and significant as that between Moses and God at the burning bush in Exodus 3. Consider the journey and the geography — the prophet's death-wish, and the final location at the very place where his illustrious predecessor had received God's Word in the Ten Commandments. And the depth of the spiritual experience recounted here makes the Word of God bitingly relevant and profoundly personal to people of faith in every generation.

The context is a time of political and religious unrest and uncertainty. The psychology of the prophet matches that of anyone who is under stress, or at a turning point in life, or who is feeling unwanted, unappreciated, unloved — in short, who considers themselves to be something of a failure. So there may be a specific reason why you need to face this question now.

Yet the same question could be relevant at any time in the course of your spiritual journey. It can be addressed just as profitably when you are feeling buoyant and satisfied with life as it is. A momentary pause, at home, on holiday, in church, or especially on retreat, may be just the right time to listen, deeply, to the Lord's challenging summons: "What doest thou here?"

Suddenly (as Elijah discovered), there can be no running away, no hiding, no self-delusion, no avoiding the naked truth. That 'still small voice' (literally in the Hebrew, 'the voice of thin silence') is insistent and penetrative. We cannot but listen. And, like the prophet, we shall be told by God to 'go' — to re-engage with the world, but in the surer knowledge that "I AM (is) with you always" (Matthew 28.20).

Birthplace

"I will judge you in the place where you were born"
(Ezekiel 21.30 NEB)

This Saying is selected from a harsh prophecy of judgement. It nevertheless gives us great reason to hope.

We were 'born' into the human race. By virtue of their baptism, Christians are 'born again' into the Church so that God's creative life and love would flow through them into this and every future generation. The 'places' where we were born, and re-born, are not just a matter of geography. There are environmental, cultural and intellectual aspects of our birth and rebirth that are held deeply within us, within the heart. That is where God also lives and where we are subject to his judgement. It is within us that he confronts us with what is right and wrong.

God created us for the purpose of setting forth his glory. He has the right to direct us towards this, even though it means he sometimes has to oppose us face to face, so to speak, in the heart. He does this especially in our prayer times. Even though we are often justifiably subjected to his 'blazing wrath,' we know it is always motivated by his unfailing love and desire that we may become what he reveals of himself within us. We need God's loving anger to arouse us to the things that matter most of all, to enable us to face both our disfigured selves and our true selves by facing him.

Even a comparatively short time of contemplative prayer in the presence of God bears much fruit. The blessings we receive are out of all proportion to what we deserve.

Ezekiel's prophecy was directed against the Ammonite people because of their idolatry and the bloodshed for which they had been responsible. *We* may not have actually shed anyone's blood, but we have almost certainly caused hurt and damage to other people. We also tend to worship a variety of false gods. To us, a rebellious people, God 'rages' creatively and lovingly, so that we may become holy as he is holy.

Blind, but now I see

"I AM the light of the world . . . receive your sight"
(John 9.5 and Luke 18.42)

The third collect in the traditional Anglican service of Evensong begins, "Lighten our darkness we beseech thee, O Lord." The old words carry us forward reassuringly into the shadows of the coming night. The new order for Evening Prayer in the Church of England's *Common Worship* has an even stronger statement of the symbolic and spiritual significance of light in its preparatory prayer:

Blessed are you, sovereign God,
our light and our salvation;
to you be glory and praise for ever.
You led your people to freedom
by a pillar of cloud by day and a pillar of fire by night.
May we who walk in the light of your presence
acclaim your Christ, rising victorious,
as he banishes all darkness from our hearts and minds.
Blessed be God, Father, Son and Holy Spirit;
Blessed be God for ever.

The first Christians were quick to relate this light/darkness symbolism to Christ. His restoring of sight to the blind is itself soon recognised as being a sign of the triumph of the light and truth of God over the dark and negative forces of evil. This is the joy of the Gospel, manifest in Jesus and continuing in his followers.

In Luke's account of the healing of the blind man, we hear the Lord's command: "Receive your sight." In order to be fully effective the gift must be received and appropriated. Such Divine riches may indeed be received, but equally they may be ignored, or rejected as Jesus himself was by those who chose to remain in blindness and ignorance.

Having ourselves 'received' this Saying, we do well to use it in intercession for those who today stubbornly choose to remain blind to the glory of God — the faithless, atheists, self-centred consumers, oppressors and abusers — all those who cause unnecessary and uncomfortable mayhem in the lives of other people.

Born Again

"You must be born from above (or *born again*)"
(John 3. 3 & 7 NRSV)

The Saying continues: "No one can see the kingdom of God without being born from above."

'Born again' has come into popular usage via the charismatic movement. It usually signifies some sort of overwhelming conversion experience. It is often borrowed for use in a non-religious context to describe some new enthusiasm: 'I am a born-again cyclist,' for example. How many of those who use the phrase, even in a religious context, recognise the two-fold challenge which the words imply. First, being born is a truly traumatic experience, often including pain, distress, and even crisis. The spiritual challenge of God's call will not be a bed of roses.

Secondly, the word 'again' can also be translated 'from above.' So this is an action which we cannot bring about by our own efforts any more than we can capture the wind, which *blows where it will*. Our part is to accept and receive, letting ourselves be re-created into true images of God who alone can bring this about.

Jesus said: "Blessed are the pure in heart for they shall see God." To be pure in heart indeed implies being born from above, but isn't this a forlorn hope, a tease? How can we possibly be pure in heart, knowing all the rubbish inside us? But the pure in heart are those who seek God, who want very much to see God. Not so much the single-minded as the single-hearted. When we pray "cleanse the thoughts of our hearts by the inspiration of your Holy Spirit, that we may perfectly love you" *(Book of Common Prayer)*, we can expect to get what we ask for.

God does of course see what is wrong with us, but even more, through love, he sees the potential in us; and he can and will draw out of us our good intentions and make them happen. No vicious circle here; instead a glorious spiral reaching up to the Kingdom.

Jesus said that the one who will enter the kingdom of heaven is the one who does the Father's will (Matthew 7.21). So we intercede, drawing others into that glorious spiral of re-birth into the kingdom of heaven.

Breath of God

"MY Spirit abides among you: fear not"
(Haggai 2.5 RSV. See also Ezekiel 37.5)

Those who follow the contemplative path will be aware of the importance of paying attention to one's breathing as a precondition for the prayer of silence. Traditionally, the breath was understood as the pathway through which the soul entered the body. Breaths come in pairs except the first breath and the last breath. At the deepest level, breath is sister of spirit. One of the most ancient words for spirit is the Hebrew word *Ruah*; this is also the word for air or wind. *Ruah* also denotes pathos, passion and emotion — a state of the soul. The word suggests that God was like breath and wind because of the incredible passion and pathos of divinity.

In the Christian tradition, the understanding of the mystery of the Trinity also suggests that the Holy Spirit arises within the Trinity through the breathing of the Father and the Son; the technical term is *spiratio*. This ancient recognition links the wild creativity of the Spirit with the breath of the soul in the human person. Breath is also deeply appropriate as a metaphor because divinity, like breath, is invisible.

The world of thought resides in the air. All of our thoughts happen in the air element. Our greatest thoughts come to us from the generosity of the air. It is here that the idea of inspiration is rooted, you inspire or breathe in the thoughts concealed in the air element. Inspiration can never be programmed. You can prepare, making your self ready to be inspired, yet it is spontaneous and unpredictable. It breaks the patterns of repetition and expectation. Inspiration is always a surprising visitor.

The dynamic of breathing also takes in the deep world of

prayer and meditation, where through the rhythm of the breath you come down into your own primordial level of soul. Through breath meditation, you begin to experience a place within you which is absolutely intimate with the divine ground. Your breathing and the rhythm of your breathing can return you to your ancient belonging, to the house, as Eckhart says, that you have never left, where you always live: the house of spiritual belonging.

Burning Question

"I came to bring fire to the earth"
(Luke 12.49 NRSV)

Jesus used these words to refer to the salvation he would bring to the world by his passion. "I came to bring fire to the earth, and how I wish it were already kindled!" We can see something of the cost of our salvation in this Saying. It is a sort of preview of the agony in the garden of Gethsemane. In the Greek myth, Prometheus *stole* fire from heaven to benefit mankind, and received a horrible punishment for doing so because Zeus did not want human beings to have this gift. The contrast with Jesus is striking, because he came to earth to fulfil God the Father's will for our salvation.

Fire is a symbol of God's power to purify, lead and comfort. "Our God is a consuming fire" (Hebrews 12.29), burning up what is evil in us because he loves us. "For he is like a refiner's fire ... he will sit as a refiner and purifier of silver, and he will purify the descendants of Levi ... " (Malachi 3. 2-3). God made himself known to Moses through the burning bush (Exodus 3) and he led the Israelites through the desert by a pillar of cloud by day and a pillar of fire by night (Exodus 13.21). The two disciples on the way to Emmaus were taught by the risen Jesus without knowing him, but they said afterwards, "Were not our hearts *burning* within us while he was talking to us on the road" (Luke 24.32).

Fire is closely connected with the Holy Spirit who came on the disciples in the form of tongues of fire on the day of Pentecost, changing them from frightened men and women who hid behind locked doors to fearless heralds of the risen Jesus. The baptism Jesus gives is a baptism with the Holy Spirit and fire (Luke 3.16). Through contemplative prayer we allow the Holy Spirit to burn away the evil in us, lead us in the way of God's commands and energise us to carry out his purposes. Through contemplative intercession we share the fire of the Holy Spirit with others.

Christmas Present

**"Whatever measure you deal out to others will be
dealt to you in return"**
(Luke 6.38 NEB)

Some of the Words of God which we contemplate reveal aspects of his Nature, such as "I AM the Holy one in the midst of thee." Some are promises or commands: "Ye shall be Holy, even as I, the Lord your God, am Holy." Some are comforting and strengthening: "I AM with you always." Some are a bit uncomfortable, or thought provoking at least, such as this one.

The picture is that of the first century grain seller in the market place. You make a purchase, and hold out your cloak to receive the grain. The grain seller can pour in the barest minimum, and possibly cut a bit off even that. Or he can be generous, almost reckless, pouring in so much that even when pressed down, it overflows. So, if our philosophy of life is "keep yourself to yourself," niggardly in giving to others of our material, or, far more importantly, our spiritual resources, we shall in turn find ourselves becoming increasingly isolated, lonely and unhappy.

Charles Dickens hit the truth in his *Christmas Carol*. Scrooge, the miser, hater of his fellow human beings, between Christmas Eve and Christmas Day is changed from unutterable meanness to a new generosity of spirit. This brought out generosity and affection in everyone he met. In his vision of himself as he was, he feared it was too late to change. But the measure he now began to deal out brought an immediate return of affection. The more we contemplate the Words of God, inevitably, the more our lives will overflow with his compassion and love.

The custom of giving presents at Christmas originates from

the Supreme Gift of God Himself to mankind, signified by the 'mangered babe' (to borrow a phrase from a memorable Christmas poem by David Lockwood). Nothing could have changed mankind more radically. For, as St Athanasius taught, the Gift of the Divine becoming human enabled the human to become Divine.

Come Along

"Come and see"
(John 1.39)

These are the words of Jesus to Andrew and another (unnamed) disciple when they asked him, "Rabbi, where are you staying?" They are repeated by Philip (verse 46) when Nathaniel rather scornfully said "Can anything good come out of Nazareth?"

The words "Come and see" really convey the essence of contemplative prayer. They first refer to the journey inwards, settling down, paying attention, leaving one's baggage at the feet of Christ and hearing his invitation, "Come to me all who labour and are heavy laden, and I will give you rest." Then they refer to the end of the journey, "and see," fixing the inward gaze on the Christ, the I AM, and holding it there, staying with him.

The Divine Invitation to "come" is to be found in many places in scripture (e.g. Isaiah 55.1-3; Luke 14.15 ff; John 7.37; John 21.12). God respects our free will and does not force himself on us. We can only know him truly as we freely respond to his gracious invitation to come into his presence. In one sense we are never out of his presence, but, as Saint Augustine said, "He is always with us, but we are not always with him."

In responding to that invitation, we get a glimpse of the vision of God which is the supreme happiness his human children can enjoy: "They shall see his face" (Revelation 22. 4). Our practice of contemplation is meant to strengthen our spiritual sight so that we may become more ready to bear the bright beams of God's love, rather as the experience of the Transfiguration prepared the Church for the revelation of God's glory seen in Christ (Luke 9. 28-36).

Philip (a disciple) said to Nathaniel (an enquirer), "Come and

see," and in that way he is a model for contemplative intercession. God's invitation is never for ourselves alone; it is always
meant to be shared with others. When we receive these words of
Jesus on behalf of others we both bring them into the circle of
God's love and also experience that love more fully ourselves
because it is essentially a shared love. To see Jesus is to have
fullness of life, so these words as intercession are appropriate for
every kind of need.

Crisis Management

"All will be thrown down . . . the birth-pangs of the new age"
(Mark 13. 2 & 8 NEB)

"One thing at least we no longer need to be told is that we are in the throes of a crisis of the most appalling dimensions. We tend to call this crisis the ecological crisis, and this is a fair description in so far as its effects are manifest above all in the ecological sphere. For here the message is quite clear: our entire way of life is humanly and environmentally suicidal, and unless we change it radically there is no way in which we can avoid cosmic catastrophe. Without such change the whole adventure of civilization will come to an end during the lifetime of many now living."

With those words, the Orthodox philosopher and theologian, Philip Sherrard, began his book, *Human Image . . . World Image*, published in 1992. Nearly 40 years previously, Robert Coulson* was writing about the inevitable collapse of what he called the first Christian civilization. Like previous civilizations, ours has borne what fruits it can and, like ripened fruit in autumn, it must fall and decay (see *Into God* pp. 15-19: the theme is taken up again and developed in his later writings).

Both authors know that the cause of this collapse, whether it is to be apocalyptic or not, is the direct result of a loss of contact with the Divine. But it is Coulson who sees more clearly that the collapse is to be interpreted in terms of the Gospel as "the birth-pangs of the new age." And in his view, it is contemplatives, focussed on God, who sow the seed for the new spiritual growth which will surely emerge following the collapse of the old order.

*Founder of The Fellowship of Contemplative Prayer

As well as its warning which is so relevant to us today, this Saying has a personal dimension. There can be a 'throwing down,' a downfall, in anyone's life. Contemplative listening to this Divine Word will help us to understand such setbacks, not as unmitigated and tragic loss, but as 'birth pangs' whose pain will actually prepare us for a new vision of God's purposes for us. An apt Word, then, for the start of a new phase in your life, or, if you are using it during January, for a new year.

Dependency

"Apart from ME you can do nothing"
(John 15.5)

These words are part of the teaching that Jesus gave to his disciples shortly before his passion. He said to them, "I AM the vine, you are the branches. If a man abides in ME, and I in him, he will bear much fruit; apart from ME you can do nothing."

In the Old Testament, Israel is often described as God's vineyard, and the prophets speak of the vine as having run wild and become degenerate so that it bears no grapes. The disciples are not to think that just because they are Jews, they are part of God's vine. Jesus is the true vine, and only by being joined to him can they bear fruit.

We depend on God for the air we breathe, the food we eat, the functioning of our bodies. He could, if he wished, withdraw any of these things. Modern society has become arrogant and individualistic; people think that they can be self-sufficient, that they can control their own destiny. It is an illusion, and it leads to despair. To regain a sense of proportion, we need to hear God saying to us, "I AM the Lord, who has made all things. I AM your redeemer, who formed you in the womb" (Isaiah 44.2). "Without ME, you can do nothing".

We also depend on God for our spiritual life. We may be involved in some kind of Christian service. At first we may feel weak and nervous, and this drives us consciously to depend on God, but as we become more confident it is very easy to forget him, to get into the habit of running under our own steam. Then we become stressed, exhausted, and ineffective. The busier we are, the more difficult it is to find time to be still before God. Cut off from him, we wither and die.

"We offer you ourselves, as an emptiness to be filled with your divine fullness." This prayer is often used at the end of a time of silent prayer. So let us allow the risen Christ to fill our emptiness, as we listen to him saying to us, "Apart from ME, you can do nothing."

Doing Nowt

"You shall do no work . . . without ME you can do nothing"
(Leviticus 23.28 & John 15.5 AV)

This composite Saying from the two Testaments is a useful example to show how our Scriptures are a unity, each Testament commenting on and interpreting the other in the light of the over-arching Word. Far from being an encouragement to idleness, the provision of the Sabbath referred to in Exodus and Leviticus as a day of rest from daily toil is a positive reminder of our human need, not only to rest, but continually to re-orientate our being in the direction of our Divine Source.

I once came across a Christian farmer in Staffordshire who persistently refused to have any work done on his farm on Sundays, apart from the essential nurturing of the animals. The local community simply looked on in astonishment, especially at harvest time when the weather was fine. The more deeply committed you are to the Word of God, the more challenging it becomes. When the Israelites were in panic at the edge of the Red Sea, Moses simply told them: "*Stand still* and see the salvation of the Lord" (Exodus 14.13).

We are told by God to "do no work" principally because "without ME, you can do nothing" — "do", that is, in the sense of "achieve." Hyperactivity is the mark of a godless generation; but all human activity which is detached from God is just so much churning of water — a lot of noise, froth and bubble, impressive to watch, perhaps, but with no really positive result in terms of usefulness.

The Bishop of St Albans wrote recently: "If I could dream a year for our Church, it would be a communications-free year . . . I mean a year of silence, a year when the whole Church could wait in stillness upon God . . . Jesus spent 30 years saying, as far as we know, nothing. The Church has spent the last 2000 years saying things endlessly. A year of self-imposed silence and stillness would be balm to our minds, bodies and souls."

The contemplative, apparently doing nothing from the human perspective, is actually living within God's 'sabbath rest.' It is here that we truly engage in spiritual 'work,' re-connecting both ourselves and those for whom we pray with the loving Divine intention. Such passivity can sanctify all other activity.

Doors Opening

"Look! I have set before you an open door"
(Revelation 3.8)

Many and varied are the messages that come to us from God. A fine selection of them is to be found in the letters to the Seven Churches of Asia in the Revelation given to John of Patmos. And they nearly all carry resonance for God's people of every age, including our own.

In this case, the letter is to the Church in Philadelphia. This city had been founded during the second century before Christ as part of the Greek empire. At the time it was a border town, standing at the place where three countries met; Mysia, Lydia, and Phrygia. Far from being a far-flung outpost, it stood in a strategic position confronting further pagan territories, the wilds of Phrygia and beyond, that were to be absorbed into the empire and imbued with Greek culture. The city also commanded one of the principal trade routes between Europe and the East. It was therefore an open door of opportunity, a kind of missionary of Hellenism to the pagan lands beyond.

This Saying, then, will have straight away found an echo in the hearts and minds of the Philadelphian Christians. The Lord commends them for their steadfastness and faith in the midst of adversity. Now he wants them to know that, whatever trials and difficulties they may have to face (one of them, 'the synagogue of Satan,' sounds pretty fearsome), these are doors of opportunity for the message of the Gospel, the message of truth and right-eousness, to be proclaimed.

There is fruitful meditation to be done if one ponders on the various 'doors' in the New Testament, the door of the heart at which Christ knocks later on in this same chapter (verse 20); the door of the sheep in John 10.7; the "door of faith for the Gentiles" in Acts 14.27, mentioned again by Paul in 1 Corinthians 16.9, 2 Corinthians 2.12 and Colossians 4.3.

As we hear these words spoken deeply within us, it may well be that God is asking us to consider what doors of opportunity are opening before us, even in the guise of setbacks and adversities.

Down to Earth

"Take MY yoke upon you, and learn of ME"
(Matthew 11.29)

The artist Harry Becker lived in Suffolk alongside impoverished workers. He drew and painted them, and their work, and the livestock in their care. One of his paintings depicts two labourers clearing a weed-choked ditch. Their job, mind-numbing and burdensome, is to keep the water flowing so that the grain crops are not flooded. Heavy land, saturated with water, will not produce the wheat.

The artist, and his models, were poor, often hungry, working in adverse conditions, wet and cold. To perform manual work (or, for that matter, to continue painting) when so hampered, requires discipline and determination — especially when the reward for the work is minimal. Becker struggled with his career; the farm workers struggled daily. We too, struggle with our faith.

These days, many people live their lives without touching the earth; they are out of touch with the seasons and with reality. But Jesus talks to us about growth, about food and crops. He uses the open-air occupations to illustrate His teaching. We must become fishers of men. We must grasp the plough and not look back. We need to take a lesson from the farmer sowing seed by hand, use our imagination and watch where the seed falls. We must consider the beauties of nature, flowers and birds, to be mindful of God's bounty. We are to look for the missing lambs.

I have been reflecting on Harry Becker's painting of the two ditchers. It makes me aware of water and of Christ the Living Water. In addition, I am strongly reminded that God's work is done by human hands: in the words of the saint, "Christ has no hands but ours." The hands of Jesus in the carpenter's shop would have fashioned many yokes, crafted to fit the shoulders of draught animals, and perhaps also for men and women carrying buckets. The call to follow him in faith will at times be burdensome for us, but never beyond our strength. Accepting his yoke means that you are provided with the necessary equipment for the task.

Ethical Energy

"Blessed are the meek, for they shall inherit the earth"
(Matthew 5.5).

'Meek' in modern speech means 'gentle' and implies weakness. But the Greek noun is *praotes*. The word is difficult to render into English. One scholar writes: "It must be clearly understood that the meekness commended to the believer is the fruit of power." The word was sometimes used for a horse that had been broken in; power under control.

"Now the man Moses was very meek..."(Numbers 12.3); but he was not always gentle. Observe for example his reaction to Aaron's golden calf (Exodus. 32.20) when "his anger waxed hot" and he threw down the tablets of the Law and broke them; he ground the idol to powder, mixed it with water and made God's people drink it.

"Gentle Jesus, meek and mild?" Not really. What about the cleansing of the temple? Or the time when Jesus proposed to heal a cripple on the Sabbath and looked round on the Pharisees "with anger" (Mark 3.5).

God's anger (or 'wrath') is not 'ratty' like mine. It has been well defined as Blazing Ethical Energy, and that describes accurately the anger of Jesus. So meekness might be understood as Ethical Energy Properly Applied, sometimes gently, but not always.

In the wilderness Jesus was tempted to turn stones into bread. Was this just a lure to a very hungry man? Not really. Jesus went hungry to experience humanity fully. But to bestow instant universal famine relief — that would be putting Ethical Energy to the test. Would it however be properly applied? No; Jesus came to do the job *within* us, not *instead of* us. Which is why he said,

"*You* give them something to eat" (Matthew 4.16). Divine Meekness delegates. Again, on the "exceeding high mountain" (Matthew 4.8), the Tempter was not dangling the bait of kingly status. Why be born lowly if that was the Father's purpose? But seeing the manifold tyrannies of the world, Jesus could have lashed out in righteous wrath to impose universal justice. That would be Ethical Energy but improperly applied. Therefore it would not be meekness.

Meekness is an infection that humans must catch from the Son of Man. It will be a slow process, much assisted by contemplating the words of God in Scripture.

Familiar Spirit

"I am with you always"
(Matthew 28.20)

Children's author Philip Pullman, in his great trilogy *His Dark Materials*, conceived the idea of the *daemon* who accompanied the characters like a familiar spirit wherever they went (except into the world of the dead). This was a kind of hidden self, an individual's *persona* or character.

God ever-present in Christ is somewhat along these lines, only much, much more. This promise at the end of Matthew's Gospel was given to the disciples of Jesus at an extraordinarily critical time. The one they had been drawn to in the three short years of his ministry, the one they had come to know, honour and love ever more deeply, the one to whom they had committed themselves body and soul: suddenly he had been snatched from them in death. Then, even more surprisingly, he had returned to them in a sort of life. And shortly after that, he was taken from them again, at least in physical terms.

This emotional roller-coaster one would think would have left them in a state of utter bewilderment and grief. But that was not the case. On the contrary, having been given a mandate to "go ... and tell," they discovered that they possessed the resources to do that, and with "great joy." This was the fulfilment of the promise made at the time of the Ascension: "I am with you always." Not, I will be, but I am. They became increasingly aware of this familiar, and totally good Spirit accompanying them at all times and in all places. He was with each one. He was in each one. And they knew he always would be, "to the end of time."

Years ago, the daughter of Stalin, Svetlana, spoke about how she became conscious of the Lord's continuing presence with her.

She was secretly baptized at the age of 37. The presence of the Lord, she said, did not depend on her being in church, which would have been a risky business for her at the time. Nor was it blotted out by the prevailing materialism and atheism with which she was surrounded.

A Wayside pulpit proclaimed, "If God seems far away, who's moved?" Use the Saying from Matthew 28.20 for yourself when God seems absent, and in intercession for others who do not know him or who need his presence.

Family Matters

**"Blessed are they who hear the Word of God, and keep it ...
and do it ...
These are MY family"**
(Luke 8.21 & 11.28)

In Judaism the family bond is strong. Jesus' behaviour as an itinerant preacher and healer caused questions to be raised about his relationship with his family. It seemed to some people that he had cut loose from them. Look up Matthew 12.46-50; Mark 3.35; Luke 2.48; John 2.4.

We can take it, however, that Jesus was not lacking in affection; his concern for his mother shown in John 19.26-27 indicates that. As usual, the unconventional behaviour of a prophet (Jesus was also a prophet) points to a spiritual truth. Our relationship with God has priority over all other relationships, however loving. More than that, those other relationships, especially the close ones within the family framework, will deepen and become all the more meaningful if our relationship with our Creator is taken seriously and nurtured. It is no coincidence that the escalation in marriage and family break-ups comes at a time when society has to a greater extent than ever before chosen to turn its back on God.

The founder of the Fellowship of Contemplative Prayer was sometimes heard to say that the Fellowship was his 'alternative family.' In no way was he lacking in affection for his natural family of whom he was very fond. He was simply making the point that those who, in all sincerity, "hear the Word, and keep it, and do it" within a fellowship of like-minded people actually forge a spiritual relationship comparable to that of a human family. Many people who have experienced a silent retreat have discovered how it seems possible to get to know other people whom you have never met before simply by sharing contemplative silence. The value of the prayer group, the quiet day, and the retreat can never be over-estimated.

When you come to ponder these two texts, You will note the specific pattern of engaging with God's Word suggested in this book. The Word is to be *heard*, but more than that, it is to be *kept*; that is, taken down into the 'heart' where it may take root (Mark 4.3-9). Then it must also be *done*; that is, our will must be brought into play to make the Word effective in daily life and in intercession.

Firmly Grounded

"Look to the rock"
(Isaiah 51.1 RSV)

It is remarkable how often the Bible uses physical language to speak about God. The Psalms frequently refer to God as a 'rock'. "Be thou my strong rock, and house of defence, that thou mayest save me. For thou art my strong rock and my castle" (Psalm 31. 2-3. See also the Psalms 18. 2 & 31; 27.5; 28.1; 42.9). 'Rock' is also sometimes used of human beings, as in the phrase "the shade of a great rock in a weary land" (Isaiah 32.2), where the reference is to a righteous king (v.1). Jesus took the metaphor and was the first to use it as a nickname when he gave it to Simon (*Petros* = rock). It is interesting to think that there were no "Peters" in the world before Simon the fisherman from Galilee was given his new name.

The complete Saying in Isaiah reads, "Look to the rock from which you were hewn, and the quarry from which you were digged. Look to Abraham your father and to Sarah who bore you." Human beings are only rocks in so far as they depend on God the rock. Our use of the phrase for contemplative prayer reminds us that we contemplate God the rock in union with a great company of people who have done so before us.

'Rock' suggests two main thoughts: protection and stability. Most of the references in the Psalms to God as the rock relate to his protecting care of us, as does Toplady's great hymn, *Rock of Ages*. It is said that Toplady was inspired to write this hymn when he was caught in a very bad storm one day and found shelter in the cleft of a rock. The other idea, stability, makes us think of walking on firm ground instead of floundering about in shifting sands. "He drew me up from the desolate pit, out of the miry bog, and set my feet upon a rock, making my steps secure" (Psalm 40.2).

The two ideas, protection and stability, are combined in our Lord's parable of the two houses, one built on rock, one on sand (Matthew 7.25). The parable is very relevant to the practice of contemplative prayer in which we not only hear the word of God, but do it.

Flood Warning

"When you pass through the waters I will be with you;
(they shall not overwhelm you)"
(Isaiah 43.2 NRSV)

This Saying was spoken by God to the prophet of the Babylonian Exile whose writings are lodged in the middle of the book of Isaiah, making a separate little book out of chapters 40 to 55. He and his compatriots were no doubt reflecting on the myth of the Great Flood which was part of a Babylonian epic. The story was based on hard practical experience of local flash floods which happened in the area from time to time.

In the Jewish mind of the first century, water in overwhelming quantities was symbolic of primal chaos and a reminder of the awe-inspiring power of the Creator. God knows that we have in this life to "pass through the waters" of turbulence and distress. His promise is that, when that time comes, he is with us. He does not undertake to lead us round the edge of the floods, or to remove the obstacles from our path. We are not promised a life free of difficulties, sorrows or failures. But we are assured of the abiding presence of God to support and sustain us so that we are not overwhelmed. Too often our gaze is fixed on the flood-waters and we quail at the sight. This Saying reminds us to set our sights on the One whom nothing can overwhelm, for he is Lord of all.

Our 'flood-waters' may be illness, suffering, bereavement, approaching death, domestic difficulties, unemployment, a sense of failure in marriage or at work, or perhaps our own turbulent emotions and attitudes. Being human is no easy task. It is not by chance that the funeral service normally includes what is arguably the best-known and best-loved poem in the world, Psalm 23. "Yea, though I walk through the valley of the shadow of death, I will fear no evil: for thou art with me, thy rod and they staff they comfort me." The Good Shepherd is not leading David the shepherd boy round the dark and dangerous valley. The assumption is that there is no way round; he must go through. And so he does, in full assurance of the One who accompanies him as he goes.

Glory Glory Hallelujah

"I will display my glory among the nations"
(Ezekiel 39.21)

Before his arrest, Jesus prayed: "Father, I desire that those whom you have given me may be with me to see my glory." The displaying of the glory of God is a theme that runs like a golden thread through the whole of the Bible. It is implicit in creation in Genesis; it is explicit in the exodus from Egypt and the giving of the law; it is experienced and written about by the prophets.

The glory of Jesus Christ comes directly from the glory of God the Father. It is revealed at the birth of Jesus; it is implicit at the time of his calling to ministry, and it becomes explicit in that ministry, in his words and loving actions. It is shown to his three closest companions on the Mountain of Transfiguration.

We are privileged to be surrounded by God's glory in the variety and beauty of our planet and in the breathtaking immensity of space. We are aware of it in the eyes of children and the love we share with one another. We experience it in the compassion of those who care and the kindness of strangers, and come close to it in the beauties of art and culture, and the patterns of science. We feel the impact of the glory of God in our acts of worship, especially in Eucharist.

But how can we possibly see God's glory in the despoiling of the environment, in children who suffer, in acts of terrorism, in starvation, oppression or genocide? The answer can only be in Christ. Bound up with the revelation of God's glory in Jesus is the glory of his courage in the acceptance of suffering, his witness for the truth, and ultimately in his dying and death on the cross. The cross is a symbol of innocence humiliated and brutalised. We became aware after World War II of how some prisoners of war and victims of Nazi oppression, although constantly humiliated and degraded, were able to witness to the redeeming power and glory of God. Here, and in other circumstances of extreme stress, we may find in faith the glory of the resurrection of Christ.

This Saying is a clear and positive statement from God of his intention for us and for the whole of creation: i.e. to be gathered into the perfectly glorious heavenly city foreseen by Saint John. "The city has no need of sun or moon, for the glory of God is its light" (Revelation 21.23).

God the Mother

"I AM the mother of beautiful love"
(Ecclesiasticus [Sirach] 24.18 NRSV margin [Apocrypha])

The complete verse reads: "I am the mother of beautiful love, of fear, of knowledge, and of holy hope; being eternal, I am given to all my children, to those who are named by him." The chapter is a hymn in praise of Wisdom; and in scripture, Wisdom is identified with the Godhead and is feminine (see Proverbs 8). Mother Julian of Norwich wrote: "As truly as God is our Father, so just as truly he is our Mother." The following words come from *The Threefold Reality* by Robert Coulson*:

"We customarily refer to God, the Word, the Christ, as He...We do well to remember that He is no less She. The Heart of I AM is His feminine, maternal aspect, as His Will is the masculine, paternal. If we call the latter His Creative Intention, we may call His maternal aspect His Creative Source, the spiritual womb in which the Idea of the knowable Reality is conceived. And since we are dealing with spiritual things, that womb is the Idea. Hence the Bible and other scriptures usually refer to Divine Wisdom and Understanding as She....From what we have said of the feminine aspect of I AM, His Heart, it is clearly the *receiving* principle in relation with the *originating* one, His Will. Now true receptivity is not merely passive, but includes the vital capacity to attract. This capacity is essentially that of

---

The Threefold Reality is one of the foundational writings of The Fellowship of Contemplative Prayer. This hardback has long been out of print, but a few copies are available. For details please consult the website of The Fellowship of Contemplative Prayer.
www.contemplative-prayer.org.uk

Beauty....So His Heart stands revealed as supremely wise and beautiful, as...his Will stood revealed as supremely loving and good."

This is to do with "the beauty of holiness" referred to in Psalms 29, 96 and 110 (see also Ezekiel 28.12).

We live in an age in which there is much ugliness, and where the portrayal of what passes for 'love' on our TV screens is far too often a bitter distortion of the godly qualities of goodness, beauty and truth. By receiving this Saying at depth into our own minds and hearts, and using our wills in intercession to share it with others, we shall be doing our bit to set the record straight in the light of the supreme Goodness, Beauty and Truth of I AM.

God's Choice

"All ... is mine ... I have chosen you"
(Psalm 50.12 & John 15.16)

The reason why I have linked these two Words from the Lord together is made clear by referring to Deuteronomy 10 verse 14-15. "Although heaven and the heaven of heavens belong to the Lord your God, the earth with all that is in it, yet the Lord ... chose you ... out of all the peoples ... today." It is certain that the Jews are a chosen people, being as it were the cradle of the Messiah, and therefore God's instrument of salvation.

Two other factors need to be stressed. First, it is also clear from Scripture that this choice (selection or election) on the part of God is not so much a privilege as a source of perpetual astonishment — that the majestic and all-powerful God of all creation should, in his loving-wisdom, have made this choice. Second, that this divine choosing is not limited to one nation or ethnic group, but is extended to all or any people of faith. We, people of faith, have been selected as part of the Divine plan for the re-newal and salvation of the whole created order.

Now, that is an awesome thought! It sends the mind oscillating between ideas of littleness and greatness; the greatness of the sovereignty of God over absolutely everything, and the smallness of our place as a speck in creation. Having pondered on that, the next thing that comes to mind is the completely upside-down way in which God works. Humanity thinks that the strong and powerful, the clever politicians and the skilful scientists and powerful military nations are the ones who will save the world. But God's way is to use the power-less and faith-full to do the job. If the world is to change for the better, then the only way is from the bottom up, not from the top down. That applies at the local level as well as on the national or international level. For it is only by conforming to the will of God that any real improvement can be made. And you or I can do that just as well as anyone else, simply by allowing the spirit and life of God's Word to flow into and through us, wherever we are and whenever we pray.

Check out Psalm 24, Exodus 19 verses 5-6 and Acts 1 verse 8 on this theme.

God's Timing

**"I still have many things to say to you but you cannot bear
them now"**
(John 16.12 NRSV)

Perhaps the point that Jesus is making in this Saying is clearer if
we slightly re-phrase the end *but you cannot bear them yet*.

It is particularly easy to make two false assumptions about
Dominical Sayings, particularly the direct words of Jesus himself.
First; that our own unaided wit will enable us to get hold of them.
Second; that we shall be ready to receive them the moment we
hear them. This is especially the case when we come to the so-
called "Hard Sayings"* — statements about loving one's enemies
(Matthew 5.44); commands to sell all you have (Mark 10.21), or to
take up your cross (Mark 8.34). But sooner or later, the corrective
that Isaiah heard will dawn on us too. Look up Isaiah 55, verses
8 and 9.

Mercifully, the Lord himself continues in this 16th chapter of St
John's gospel to indicate a progressive revealing; the work of the
Holy Spirit who will guide us into all truth, and thus to what will
rightly bring glory.

This means that all too often it is only in the light of
experience, in the patience of oft-repeated contemplation and
supremely in our handling of suffering that difficult Sayings
begin to make sense to us.

The great Orthodox contemplative, Father Sophrony, out of a
lifetime of prayer, especially his time as a solitary on Mount
Athos for most of the Second World War, said that what

---

*There is a useful book by F.F.Bruce called *The Hard Sayings of Jesus*.
Hodder & Stoughton 1983.

happened to the Lord will, in growing measure, be our lot also. "The cup which I drink, you shall indeed drink" (Mark 10.39). Yet in the very anguish of whatever lies ahead we shall find we have the benefit of the prayer of Jesus to his Father: "I have given them the words which Thou gavest me, and they have received them, and have come to know, surely, that I came from Thee . . . and the glory which Thou hast given me I have given them" (John 17. 8 & 22).

And in this "glory" and this bearing of His life-giving words we are more than conquerors through Him who loved us.

God's True Name

"I AM . . . this is MY Name for ever"
(Exodus 3. 14-15 REB)

Christmas is the precise moment in the year when we should be enabled to focus or re-focus energetically on God. But alas! Most of us find exactly the opposite happening. As Wordsworth wrote: "The world is too much with us . . . getting and spending we lay waste our powers." In the midst of so many distractions, it is really important to make the best of the Advent season with its message of challenge and judgement. So we try, during the consumerist run-up to the Festival, in our prayer groups and in our quiet times, to keep alive within us the reality of God . . . God who is the super-essential transcendent Divine mystery above all, through all, and in all. There is no better way of doing this than to hear again that foundational Word of Self-revelation given to Moses at the Burning Bush: "I AM . . . this is MY Name for ever."

In the 10th chapter of the Bhagavad Gita (Penguin Classics edition), Arjuna, the questioner, praises God (revealed to him as Krishna) thus: "Supreme Brahman . . . unborn God . . . Lord of all . . . I have faith in all thy words, because these are words of truth." The Divine response comes in a glittering array of I AM Sayings, many of which are similar, if not identical, to those in St John's Gospel and in Revelation. "I dispel darkness by the light of wisdom . . . I AM the prayer of silence . . . I AM the tree of life . . . I AM the beginning and the middle and the end of all that is . . ." All this leads to a climactic conclusion. "Know that with one single fraction of MY Being I pervade and support the universe, and know that I AM."

As we are once again drawn to meditate on that "single fraction" of God's Being cradled in the manger, let us, as best we may, quieten the clamour of the world and of our own senses, and listen at depth to His utterance of the Divine Name in this Saying. By so doing, we shall have a better chance of side-lining the commercial world, and of understanding more deeply the crucial significance of the Festival of the Incarnation and the person of the Word-become-Flesh.

God-Space

"This is my resting place for ever; here I will make my home"
(Psalm 132.14 NEB)

This verse from the Psalms of David refers to the temple which stood at the heart of Jerusalem. God says of the temple that it is his 'desire' to make it his permanent dwelling-place. But since AD70 there has been no temple. So what is the meaning of this Saying?

The New Testament asserts that "you are the temple" (2 Corinthians 6.16). You are God's resting place for ever; in you he wills to make his home. The word *temple* is connected with the word *contemplation*; con-*templ*-ation. So contemplation is precisely about allowing yourself to be the temple, to be the place in which God can rest and make himself at home, the place in which he can live and work and have his being.

Contemplation is a powerful tool, enabling us to "build on the foundation laid by the apostles and prophets" with Christ Jesus himself as the foundation stone. "In him (says Saint Paul in Ephesians 2. 19-22) the whole structure grows into a holy temple." In con-*templ*-ation we are built into a spiritual dwelling for God.

King Solomon built his temple to the glory of God, paying special attention to the inner sanctuary, the most holy place, the Holy of Holies. Everything in it was made or overlaid with pure red gold. Throughout Christian history, church buildings, especially of the Catholic and Orthodox traditions, have been constructed richly and entirely to the glory of God, with special attention paid to the sanctuary, the most holy place.

You are the temple. Everything you are and everything you do is intended for the glory of God. In particular, your own 'inner sanctuary', your own 'most holy place,' is to be a heart of gold.

If, in your times of contemplation, you allow the Words and Sayings of God to cut their way to your innermost thoughts and desires, your most holy place will become pure gold. Contemplative experience testifies to the truth of the Psalmist's words: "The words of the Lord are pure words, like silver refined in a crucible, like gold seven times purified" (Psalm 12.6). Allow yourself to be filled, in the silence with the pure gold of God's Words.

Good For You

"I will make all my goodness pass before you"
(Exodus 33.18 NEB)

The biblical view of God's goodness has four elements:

1. God is good *in Himself*: morally perfect. This is the basis for all Jewish and Christian (and other) teaching on moral goodness: because God is good. Psalm 100: "The Lord is good and his love is everlasting; his constancy endures to all generations." Contemplating the supreme glory of God's perfection, we apply the word 'good' for acknowledging worth. Jesus asserts, "No one is good except God alone" (Mark 10.18). People and things are good, only in so far as they derive from and conform to the goodness of God.

2. The *works* of God are good. "God saw everything that he had made, and it was very good" (Genesis 1.31). We are the crown of his creation, made in his glorious image. Reflect on the world of nature, especially human nature, which in spite of its many flaws, sometimes reveals, in its thinking and feeling and action, something of the glorious goodness of God. As a wise priest once said: "You cannot account for some people, unless God exists."

3. The *gifts* of God are good. They express his unlimited generosity and are beneficial, causing the well-being of those who receive them. He showers us with gifts, and a secret of a truly joyful life lies in the disciplined counting of blessings, including the mixed and disguised blessings. God's goodness is always passing before us.

4. The *commands* of God are good (Psalm 119.39), and they are for our good. St Paul says that "the commandment is holy and

just and good" (Romans 7.12) and "let your whole nature be transformed; then you will be able to discern the will of God, and to know what is good" (Romans 12.2). In contemplative prayer, we make good use of the loving commands of God in the use of such Sayings as "Be fruitful," "Do not be afraid," "Live always in my presence," "You shall be holy," "Be attentive to every word of mine." Obey any one of them and the path of rich blessing is marked out for you.

Good Lord

"I will deliver thee . . . for Mine own sake"
(2 Kings 20.6 AV)

Have you ever stopped dead in your tracks, either physically, or mentally, or emotionally, and wanted to throw yourself down on the ground in utter wonderment, praise and love of God, because of something beautiful you have seen, heard or thought? It is happening to me all the time. Because God is revealing Himself to you and to me. The unexpected is the most thrilling. The burning bush, for example, which Moses came across (Exodus 3).

The Bible might well be called 'The Book of Surprises,' with Jesus as the biggest surprise of all; the disciples on the mount of the Transfiguration, in amazement at the sight of the Lord, familiar yet utterly changed before their eyes (Luke 9.38). The centurion who asked Jesus to heal his servant felt unworthy to approach Jesus (Matthew 8.8).

This sort of thing happens all the time when we are living in the presence of God. Bishop Hugh Montefiore called his autobiography "O God, what next!" He was constantly astonished at what God was up to. A modern worship song has Saint Peter saying to Jesus, "What next, whatever next!"

God reveals himself as the one who cares, regarding us with continuing loving-kindness. He *is* caring for us, supporting and giving, meeting our needs even before we are aware ourselves of what our needs really are. Take a look at Psalm 65 verses 1 to 9. "We shall be satisfied with Thy goodness." Here we are moving from the nature of God to what he does because of who he is. He delivers us. Have you ever fully realised how there is nowhere, no time, nor any situation, when God's compassion (his *compassion*, passion = feeling, com = togetherness) and love will not rescue us when we need to be delivered, and re-establish us when we fall?

Look at 1 Corinthians 2. 9-10. "No eye has seen . . . what God has prepared for those who love Him." This also is wonderful. He has *already prepared* goodness for you and me. That is what is called "the depths of God" in verse 10.

Even in the midst of tribulation, let us try to continue in thankfulness for the blessings we receive and have received, and the love outpoured and the renewal offered "for Mine own sake."

Hallowed be thy Name

**"My people will hallow my name,
when they see what I have done in their nation"**
(Isaiah 29.23 NEB)

In contemplative silence the use of this Word from the Lord reveals an astonishing range of meaning. To begin with, to "see" what God has done requires insight, spiritual eyes. Day by day we are fed, indeed surfeited, with facts from the mass media about what is happening in our nation. But few people have the insight to see what the Lord God has done and is doing. The prophet, who habitually "hallows" the Name of God under *all* circumstances, sees His hand at work in the nation, always. Have we the insight to see that God has made us a multi-racial nation, that He has deprived us of the former "glories" of the British Empire, that He has scourged us with wars, unemployment, financial unrest, terrorism and the drug problem? Or do we have the insight to see that He has blessed us with natural beauty in our land, with the arts, with widespread spiritual renewal, with freedom from oppression and tyranny, and with the means to raise the poor out of the miseries of urban deprivation?

This Word came to mind as I watched children at play. The children I saw in the park were hallowing God's Name by nature, as it were, in their privileged innocence. In maturity, with the stains of experience upon us, we find it more difficult to hallow God's Name in our work-a-day world of domestic chores, job, travelling and making and nurturing relationships. This is why we must work harder to "receive" God's Word and put it to work in the "hallowing" process of prayer.

It is as we persevere in contemplative praying and inter-cession that we gain insight to see what the Lord has done, and is doing, in our midst ('in our midst' is an alternative translation for 'in their nation'). In this way we are helping the Church to guide the nation in true spirituality. This is not merely thanking God for the good things which we have received for our comfort. Authentic spirituality is having the insight to see that all things whatsoever are infused with God's glory, so that hallowing His Name is literally the very best thing we can do, under *any* circumstances.

Handprint

"I have written your name on the palms of my hands"
(Isaiah 49.16 TEV)

The picture of God's hands is a common one in the Bible. In creation, God is like a master-craftsman, fashioning the world and all that is in it, including ourselves. His mighty hand and outstretched arm is seen in the works of nature as well as in the rise and fall of nations and empires. Christian devotion often likes to focus on the hands of Jesus. Children in their Sunday Schools and Bible classes make handprints as part of their project work, and learn about the hands-on ministry of the Lord, who blessed their Palestinian counterparts with his hands. Nor was Jesus averse to touch the sick and the unclean, or extend the hand of friendship to outsiders.

This rather peculiar Saying comes from the unknown prophet in exile, the one the scholars call *Deutero-Isaiah*, Second Isaiah, to distinguish him from the veritable Isaiah who lived 100 years earlier, into whose book the Second Isaiah's writings were inserted. The picture has been adapted from a practice which the Jewish exiles would have come across in Babylon. The Babylonians were in the habit of tattooing the name of the god they worshipped on their hand, in order to remind them to whom they belonged, and who was the controlling power in their lives. Here, however, the picture is turned upside-down, so to speak. We are given instead a picture of God (Israel's God; the one true God-of-gods) showing Israel that he has her name inscribed not just on one but actually on both of *his* hands.

This is a moving picture of divine grace. God's people are suffering because they have been forgetful of God. The prophets make it clear that present turmoil, anguish and upset are a consequence of people's having wilfully misinterpreted their religion to suit their own ends rather than to proclaim God's glory. Or, worse still, they had lost touch with the divine Source altogether. We have seen this happen in Western civilization during the past 200 years, to our cost and the world's detriment.

God, however, does not change. And this picture of the inscription of his people on his hands shows that, come what may, he will never abandon those children whom he loves so dearly and so permanently, both collectively and individually.

Hard Times

"I will go before you and make the crooked places straight"
(Isaiah 45.2 AV)

This Word, like many others in Isaiah, is appropriate to those times when we are faced with life's difficulties. God assures that that he goes ahead of us, smoothing the way and making things easier. For me, experience has proved the truth of his Word.

When I look back on any tough patch in my life, I can see that the 'crooked places' were really the 'kinks' or the accumulated effect of my own distorted mental and emotional attitudes. The materialistic standards to which I am continually subjected by, for example, the news and entertainment media, have adversely affected my judgement.

Contemplative prayer allows access to the Lord's infinite capacity to massage away those 'crooked places' or 'kinky' attitudes. He does this gently and patiently.

Each time I place myself in his hands, especially by the practice of contemplative prayer, he brings a change or maturing of outlook. Other people become easier to live with and the impact of difficulties is lessened. This is especially the case when, in the intercessory part of my prayer time, I bring this Word to bear on difficult people or situations.

The words 'I will go before you' imply that he is leading me towards a goal. God's goal for each human being is well known: that is, to achieve the full stature of Christ, to become fully developed as a spiritual being, to become as I AM (see Ephesians 4.13).

As God massages away each 'crooked place' from my mind, heart and whole being, I am taken a further 'straight' step towards that glorious and majestic goal.

Try to take this Saying, or part of it, as a Watchword in day-to-day affairs. At a time when you have a gap, waiting to commence the next task, or meet the next person, just focus for a brief moment on the words of promise being spoken to you from the Divine source: *I will go before you.* Then carry on, knowing that this is indeed the truth. The Lord I AM is there before you, in this or that situation, or relationship.

Head Wind

"Take heart; it is I; do not be afraid"
(Mark 6.50 NRSV)

Historically, the story of Jesus walking on the water is as shrouded in mystery as it is surrounded by incredulity. But set aside the problems of history and we are blessed with an enduring story of divine encouragement and hope. Who of us has not felt at some time in life that we were struggling against a head wind and making no progress at all? Who of us has not experienced the fearsome feeling of a threat that seems about to overwhelm us? And if by God's grace you have been spared such terrors, have a thought for the moment that will mark the ending of your earthly life. At that point you will indeed be entering uncharted waters.

We may be feeling at this very moment that a head wind is blowing and that we are 'labouring at the oars.' In spite of every effort we are getting nowhere. Perhaps things are awry with someone we love; or we are toiling at unrewarding work. Maybe we are trying to recover from an illness and seeming to make no progress. At such a time this Saying from the Lord may become the centre of our attention; and the more receptive we become, hearing the Word spoken in deep silence, the more his living presence becomes as real as it was to the fishermen on the Sea of Galilee.

I was once seriously ill and on top of the illness came a bad drug reaction. Having neither eaten nor barely slept for a week I feared death was not far away, and my tired brain was hallucinating. Happily, the corner was turned, and as I recovered, I felt the most astonishing sense of peace and security and the loving presence of God. The words of this Saying, I then knew, were literally true. I could take heart: there was no need to fear. He was present.

Significantly, the words "It is I" are the Greek *ego eimi*, the I AM declaration that you find scattered through the gospel of John; the very Name of God revealed to Moses and used so effectively by Jesus. So just four words will suffice as a watchword: "Fear not...I AM."

Heartfelt

"I will give you a heart of flesh"
(Ezekiel 36.26)

In contemplating the Word of God, we deliberately reflect the threefold reality of God who is AllLove-AllWisdom-AllPower. This means that we receive the Word into the mind, then more deeply into the heart, before expressing it by means of the will (see the Postscript at the end of this book).

The heart is the scene of God's ultimate self-revelation. In creating animal life he begins with bodies (the primitive animates), then develops brains (the higher animates), and finally, as if it were only yesterday, God reveals the heart. The 'Adam event' in evolution is the birthday of the heart.

But the Adam/Human heart is still 'a heart of stone.' Its tendency is not to hear, or want to hear, the Word of God. Which is why the psalmist says, "Today (i.e. every day), if you would hear his voice, harden not your hearts" (Psalm 95.8). We harden the heart, refusing and resisting the voice of God, because it is easier to follow the promptings of body and brain alone which, left to themselves, obey laws from an earlier stage in evolution. But in choosing the heart of stone, we paralyse and petrify the very thing which makes us distinctively human.

It is only when we open the heart to the Word, when the Word becomes flesh, that a human being becomes a true blend, a true balance and integration of body, brain and heart, a true threefold reality imaging God his maker.

The 'Christ event' was and is God's response to Adam's/Humanity's stony heart, to everything that is inhuman, brutal, destructive. Christ is the 'New Adam event', enabling the revelation of God in any and every human heart. So the contemplative discipline of silently allowing the Word to speak to the heart enables the 'heart of stone' to become a 'heart of flesh,' a warm, throbbing, loving humanity.

The heart of stone will always remain dominant so long as there is no consciousness of the Christ, the I AM, within. However, in spite of all human resistance, rebellion and disobedience, even in the face of apparent intransigence and impossibility, the heart of flesh will triumph. Why and how? Simply because "the Word was made flesh and dwelt among us, full of grace and truth" (John 1.14).

Holiday Time

"Come with me by yourselves to some lonely place where you can rest"
(Mark 6.31 NEB)

Saint Luke records more than once in his gospel how Jesus went apart to pray early in the morning, usually to be quite alone. Here Saint Mark quotes this interesting Saying where Jesus is inviting his close companions to go along with him to some quiet spot to get some rest.

There are three matters in the context of Mark's 6th chapter which make these words significant for us:

1. Earlier on we hear the unsavoury story of the murder of John the Baptist, a fellow prophet to Jesus and as likely as not a blood relation. This report must have been a great blow to Jesus and perhaps a sign of what was likely to happen to him, a kind of warning. So the natural reaction is to go aside for a while and rest, to think and reflect and pray. That is often helpful for us as well when we receive bad news that affects us deeply.

2. There is also in this chapter a record of two dramatic nature miracles, the feeding of the five thousand and the stilling of the storm when Jesus walks on the sea of Galilee. Then come works of healing. Jesus is seen to be closely involved spiritually with the creative and re-creative work of God his father. The time of withdrawal and refreshment in advance of this was an essential preliminary. We also know how helpful a holiday can be in advance of some new and demanding task. Holidays are also meant to be holy-days.

3. Jesus is practically mobbed by the crowds. He needs to get

away. He cannot give and serve without first receiving God's power and love by means of contemplative praying. So too with us; activity, however holy and good, without passivity, achieves little that is worth while.

There is a natural rhythm to the religious life; advance and retreat; withdrawal and then launching out. Like work and sleep, the one leads to the other; the one feeds on the other; both are needed. Silence, stillness and listening are powerful strengtheners, a re-newing of spiritual energy for whatever lies ahead. God's Word in this Saying may be suggesting that it is time for you to think about attending a quiet day or a retreat.

Holy God

"You shall be holy: for I, the Lord your God, am holy"
(Leviticus 19.2 NRSV)

These are words given to Moses to pass on to the people of Israel. The Lord had been offering a variety of ways for the people to conduct themselves following their return from exile in Egypt. Freedom is one thing, the exercise of freedom is another. A people getting on with building a new way of life were to hear about their relationship with the Lord. They were to be a holy people. We affirm this in our Creeds when we say "I believe in the Holy Catholic Church."

Our concern is to remain faithful when those around us appear to have forgotten God. So many people seem to be over-concerned about their own private worlds. In their relationship with others, they appear far too eager to be claiming what they presume to be their rights, and insufficiently mindful of the commandment to love and care for others. Into such a situation, seemingly to a remnant, the Lord says, "You shall be holy."

We may ask, what are the sort of qualities that make a person holy? It is perhaps easier to review the opposite. In Mark 7. 21-22 Jesus lists a brief catalogue of *un*-holy things that have their origin within the human heart: fornication, theft, murder, adultery, avarice, wickedness, deceit, licentiousness, envy, slander, pride, folly. Such things have no part in the nature of God I AM, and they defile the children made in his image and whom he never ceases to love. Against these Saint Paul's list of the 'fruits of the Spirit' in Galatians 5.22 stands the test of time: love, joy, peace, patience, kindness, generosity, gentleness, and self-control. Like the prophets of old, Paul expresses his impatience with the conventional rules and regulations of official religion. The summary in Micah 6.8 says it all: "What does the Lord require, but to do justly, to love mercy, and to walk humbly with God."

True holiness is more a matter of relationship than of private morality. The more deeply we listen to this Word from the Lord, the more likely we are to want to avoid un-holiness in our relationship with other people.

In your intercessions, remember in particular those who are called to lead God's people into holiness.

Inside Out

"I, the Lord, look on the heart"
(1 Samuel 16.7)

Although very slightly adapted, this is a true Saying from the Lord as the context makes clear, and as relevant now as it was when Samuel heard it. The prophet's God-given task was to anoint a new king. Led to the family of Jesse, his first choice was the tall, good-looking and mature son Eliab. Then God spoke. "Do not look on his appearance or the height of his stature, because I have rejected him. For the Lord does not see as mortals see. They look on the outward appearance, but the Lord looks on the heart."

Samuel was challenged, as we are challenged, to see from God's viewpoint and not from that of the world, so that we may be open to the guiding wisdom of God, of whose plans we are only dimly aware. Samuel was influenced, as we are, by outward appearances. But God's choice for king happened to be the smallest and least significant of Jesse's sons. David was chosen, not for his perfection, but because through him God's plan and promises would be fulfilled.

God takes no account of our achievements or sense of self-importance. More significantly, he can see 'the heart;' he is aware of our failings and weaknesses, but also of our potential, of what we were created to be, of what we will become. For that reason, he lovingly accepts us as we are.

It is important to review how this works out with respect to our relationship with other people. We often make judgements about others without real knowledge, without "looking on the heart." We are consequently prone to judge unjustly, perhaps even doing so to mask our own failures and prejudices. Unlike

God, we all too often are lacking in compassion and under-standing when considering the failings and weaknesses of others.

As we let this Saying dwell more deeply within us, there should be two things happening. First we should become aware, perhaps sorrowfully aware, of our own shortcomings. Second, we should become less judgmental of other people, and more aware that they, like us, are created in God's image, and that he looks on their hearts as well as ours, and knows the potential of each one of his children.

Just Right

"Neither do I condemn you"
(John 8.11 NRSV)

'Condemnation' is an Old Testament concept. God was seen as special to the Jews, to whom he was bound by a mutual contract. If they observed the contract, so they thought, the Jews would be the master-race, and the Gentiles condemned for being Gentile unless they subserved the Jews.

Thus the Old Testament put God in the role of capricious boss. In this light, God was assumed to rule the world, as earthly rulers then did (and largely still do) by a threefold system of power, fear and favourites. The fear element was the fear of condemnation.

As humans, in fact, we rather like that system. We compete for the Lord's favours, as did James and John (Mark 10. 35-44). But Jesus would have none of it. All alone, he proclaimed a new contract with God which didn't cancel the old contract but cancelled the element of fear and condemnation. This is something the conventional ruling classes in first century Palestine did not want. Coveting their assumed role as God's favourites, they crucified their God for proclaiming a new contract with humanity.

However, Jesus refused to condemn even his crucifiers. He was raised to the heavenly life on the far side of death, and as Paul famously wrote, there is now no condemnation for those who are in Christ Jesus (Romans 8.1). In this, Paul simply amplified the saying of Jesus himself in John 3.17. The New Testament is plain and simple: God does not condemn.

Non-condemnation is equivalent to salvation. Anyone may apply. There are no racial, cultural or social barriers, and it sounds easy. Indeed it is, but for one condition: we must drop our habit of condemning others, whether people known to us personally, or even wicked people we see on television. Instead, we are to be ministers of salvation, because that is what being 'in Christ Jesus' really means. This ministry is carried out by intercessors, that is to say, by those who are 'in Christ' for others.

Kids Stuff

"Change and become like little children"
(Matthew 18.3 NIV)

This is a Saying distilled from "Unless you become like little children you will never enter the kingdom of heaven."

What are the marks of a little child in this Saying of Jesus? Here is a quotation from Rowan Williams: "When adults cease to act like infants, children can once again be children." What is the difference between an infant and a child? What is it about the infant that I must change from?

Infant love is all 'need-love;' there is as yet no consciousness of love as *giving*. There is a marvellous instinct throughout the animate Creation to respond gladly to infants' needs, but it doesn't last forever. Wise parents encourage independence, and another child may well come along. And these changing circumstances serve a good purpose, because the infant must 'change and become a child,' with a growing sense of giving and sharing rather than simply demanding. In a sense, an infant is faultless, and a child is not. Yet the infant must change and learn to undertake the painful journey of cause and effect, and begin to take responsibility within the family and community. Rowan Williams' comment aptly connects with this Saying from the Lord.

Since World War Two, we have experienced in Britain a proper re-distribution of wealth; but at the same time there has appeared a culture of blame and litigation. Politicians are accused of bringing about a nanny-state; and indeed it does seem that, as a nation, we have regressed to a kind of adult infancy. People are being spoon-fed by bureaucracy with what is little more than common sense. Therefore change is needed, from infancy (in this sense) to childhood. Spiritually, human beings are required to move along the road, along the journey 'into God.' In order to do this, we must graduate from 'need-love' towards 'give-love,' moving from demand and dependency towards self-reliance and generosity. And when our journey is at an end, and we truly enter into God's kingdom, we shall have become, strangely, a kind of complete and finished 'child.' Truly God's children.

In using this Saying in contemplative intercession, we shall be helping other adults to move from adult infancy towards the discovery of being an 'adult child.' And this, we trust, will help children and young people not to be thrust back into infancy by the example of their elders.

King of Kings

"MY kingdom is not of this world"
(John 18.36)

The story of Easter is in some ways the story of a power struggle in which the forces of evil would seem to be triumphant. In fact, we are challenged by the cross and the empty grave of Jesus to re-interpret in every age questions of economic and political power in the light of what we, people of faith, understand as God's kingly rule, i.e. his kingdom. Here are some words from William Temple's commentary on St John's Gospel, indispensable background reading for a devotional approach to scripture.

Pilate is puzzled. He knew that the charge was to be one of sedition; but it has not been made; and the prisoner does not look like the leader of a serious revolution. Pilate does not constitute his court, but questions the prisoner himself . . . "Are you the king of the Jews?" . . . "You?" — the pronoun is placed so as to be most emphatic . . . The Lord's reply takes up what is the real charge, that he claims to be the Son of God, the Messiah (John 19.7; cf Mark 14.61-2). In that sense he does claim to be the 'King of Israel' (John 1.49). But he has trans-formed the conception of that messianic kingship. He has royalty, but not what the world means by royalty, for it neither proceeds from the world nor is recognisable by the world. "My kingdom is not from here . . . from this world." He does not claim a kingdom, but acquiesces in that description of his realm. It is a special kind of kingdom . . . An earthly king depends for any effective authority upon the loyal support of his people and the force they can offer in his support. The Messiah derives his authority from God alone. The quality of an earthly kingdom is, partly at least, the maintenance of order by the forcible coercion of malcontents . . . But the divine kingdom cannot be content with this. It must control not only outward conduct, but hearts and wills. Its authority is from God, who is Love; its actuality is in the willing obedience of those whose love has been called out in response to the manifested love of God. Consequently it can never fight for its 'vital interests.' because by fighting it betrays them . . . The kingdoms which are 'from this world' rest in part upon falsehood — the false but necessary supposition that the State really acts in the interest of the whole community; whereas in fact it always acts primarily in the interest of that section of the community which is able in practice to work its machinery . . . But the kingdom of God rests on truth . . . where the 'righteous Father' is supreme.

Known by Name

**"Take courage ... for the One who named you will
strengthen you"**
(Baruch 4.30 Apocrypha)

A correspondent wrote to me in some distress because of difficult
family circumstances and long-term relationship problems.
Before attempting to reply, I prayed for help for the correspondent and guidance for myself. Later the same day, I was able
to reply in the following terms:

By chance, my Scripture reading this morning took me into a
lesser-known corner of the Bible. There I read the words,
"Take courage (O Jerusalem) for the One who named you will
comfort you." This echoed another Saying, from Isaiah 43
verse 1, "I have called you by name, you are mine," which the
prophet underlines quite heavily in chapter 45 verses 3-4.

These Sayings (and others like them) relate to the exile
experience, which is analogous to times of stress in the life of
any person or community. At such times, it appears that we
are singled out for sorrow. But it is then that the Lord may
remind us that he knows us 'by name' — that is, not just as a
segment of creation, but as individuals who (if they did but
know it) are in a deep spiritual relationship with the God of
love, whose own Name is I AM.

I cannot sensibly comment on your difficult situation, and
to give advice would be foolish. Reading your letter, I couldn't
help thinking of the *seven* years that Jacob had to undergo for
the love of Rachel, and then, thinking that he had done his
stint, having to do another seven years before finding release.
All in God's plan, as it turned out.

I can't see that I have been of any great assistance; but at least some contemplative listening and hanging on to the Saying might help you to gain a little perspective in the situation, knowing that these Words are truly 'spirit and life,' and that they refer, not just to yourself, but to each member of the family whether they know it or not. "Take courage . . . for the One who named you will strengthen you". There is no need to reply to this, but if you want to, then please feel free do so after a lapse of time during which you have let this Saying enter into the mind, heart and will in times of silent prayer.

Law Abiding

"I will write My law in your heart"
(Jeremiah 31.33 NIV adapted)

This Saying, slightly adapted, is taken from a passage in Jeremiah. God is speaking to Israel. The covenant which he made with them has been broken by their disobedience, and he promises to make a new covenant with them. Instead of an external law, imposed from without, he will give them an internal law, written in their hearts. This is what he says:

"I will put my law in their minds and write it in their hearts. I will be their God, and they will be my people. No longer will a man teach his neighbour, or a man his brother, saying, 'Know the Lord', for they will all know me, from the least of them to the greatest. For I will forgive their wickedness and will remember their sins no more." Six hundred years later this prophecy came to fulfilment in the coming of Jesus at the first Christmas.

In the Sermon on the Mount, Jesus speaks about the law. Over the years it had been interpreted by the Scribes and the Pharisees to create a detailed list of rules, but the spirit of the law had been lost. Jesus gives his own interpretation:

"You have heard that our forefathers were told, 'You shall do no murder' — but I say that you shall not hate. You have heard that they were told 'An eye for an eye and a tooth for a tooth' — but I say that you are not to retaliate. Let your 'yes' be 'yes' and your 'no' be 'no'. Go the extra mile. Give and lend without reserve. Love your enemies and pray for them."

It is this law which God promises to write in the hearts of his people. James in his Epistle calls it the perfect law of liberty. How wonderful it would be if we could live spontaneously according to this pattern. To obey the spirit of the law, as Jesus explained it, requires a complete change of heart. It is not something we can do for ourselves. God promises to do it for us, if we will let him.

"I will be their God, and they will be my people. They will all know me, from the least to the greatest." This speaks to us of relationship. Instead of struggling to keep a list of rules, we have to admit our inability to keep God's law; we have to make time to listen to God; we have to clear out the clutter and make space for him so that he can write his law within us — his perfect law of liberty. Our times of stillness and listening in God's presence are opportunities for that perfect law to fill our minds and be written by God in our hearts.

Lifestyle

"Consider your way of life"
(Haggai 1.5 NEB)

These words were originally represented as coming from God, through Haggai the prophet, to Zerubbabel, Governor of Judah, and to Joshua, the High Priest. The people had returned from exile and had lived in Jerusalem for some years. They lived prosperously in well-built houses. But the Temple, the very heart of the community, still lay in ruins. Haggai speaks the Word of the Lord: "My people, why should you be living in well-built houses while my Temple lies in ruins: Consider your way of life." It seems to me that these words are currently as relevant and as penetrating as they were in 520 BC. Consider your way of life. I am thinking of the stark contrast between our comparatively prosperous externals, and our personal poverty and ruin. I am thinking of *myself* as the 'Temple' — of the way I have allowed myself to go to rack and ruin. I am meant to stand as a monument to the glory of God and to be used for his service. But if I am honest with myself, I am bound to ask why I should live so well while the thing that really matters is nothing but an old ruin, due to my neglect.

Many wise spiritual leaders have stressed the importance of being as physically fit as possible. The body is the temple of the Holy Spirit, according to Saint Paul (1 Corinthians 3.16). Consider your way of life! Your eating and drinking habits; your working life; your sleeping and recreation. Consider your way of life! Your attitudes and your relationships; the way you think about other people; the way you look at them, speak to them, touch them. Consider your way of life! Consider above all your relationship to God; the disciplines that enable you to stay close to God; your commitment to worship and prayer, fellowship and care, witness and mission. Consider your way of life! Whether you are doing what you believe God wants you to do; whether you are being obedient to his call.

There is no part of our life which can escape the penetrating, searching, probing power of the Word. "Before God no creature is hidden, but all are naked and laid bare to the eyes of the One to whom we must render an account" (Hebrews 4.13).

Lift High the Cross

"I ... lifted up from the earth, will draw all (men) unto me"
(John 12.32 AV. See also John 6.44 & 8 28)

This part of St John's Gospel is a meditation on the meaning of the death of Christ. Like St Paul, St John sees this death as having significance, not only for individual believers, but for the whole cosmos, and within creation specifically and especially for all human beings. This is a tremendous paradox. It is not surprising that people find it hard to come to terms with the idea of a crucified God. There seems to be a contradiction: ultimate goodness and ultimate badness coming together in violence. How can God let such a thing happen? There is no simple answer; there has never been a simple answer to the problem of evil, and if somebody gives you one, treat it with suspicion.

The most satisfactory approach is to be found in the mystical tradition — a way of understanding the world which reaches back through the millennia of human existence. It is an axiom of the religious mystical tradition that creation, which appears to us to be fragmentary, is in fact a unity, and that God is drawing all its diversity into unity in Himself. The focus for this unity is the Divine/Human being referred to in the writings of many religions, and acknowledged in the Bible as Christ/Messiah or Son of Man (Daniel 7.13; Revelation 1.13). Our closest contact with him is Jesus.

However, St John will not allow us to stay with the earthly Jesus. He is to be "lifted up from (literally 'out of') the earth." His death, therefore, is an exaltation. Through the degradation of earthly and earthy pain and mortality, we are to glimpse the glory — the drawing together of all diversity into glorious union with God, the Source, Guide, and Goal of all creation.

The process is beautifully expressed in an ancient prayer from the Gelasian Sacramentary:

O God of unchangeable power and eternal light, look favourably on thy whole Church, that wonderful and sacred mystery; and by the tranquil operation of thy perpetual providence carry out the work of man's salvation; and let the whole world feel and see that things which were cast down are being raised up, and things which had grown old are being made new, and all things are returning to perfection through him from whom they took their origin, even Jesus Christ our Lord.

In intercession, we reflect this Word of glorious hope towards people and situations where life is fragmented and hope seems all but lost.

Look This Way

"Look to ME and be saved"
(Isaiah 45.22 NEB)

These were words spoken by God through the unknown prophet of the Exile to the peoples of the world. This prophetic book was inserted by the old biblical editors into the middle of Isaiah where they now form the chapters 40 – 55. Two centuries before, another prophet, praying in the temple, had clearly heard God calling out amid the heavenly host: "Who will go for us, and whom shall we send?" There and then, taking his courage in his hands, Isaiah replied: "Here am I. Send me."

Like his predecessor, the prophet of the Exile vividly realised his own and his people's utter unworthiness. He became the channel to his nation of the Word of God, the I AM. He saw that rulers and people alike had come adrift from their spiritual and moral roots. Selfishness and greed had got control. There was no longer justice, or compassion, or caring for the helpless and the weak. Inevitably, ruthless violence spread like cancer. The rulers looked first to this, then to that alliance to appease the rising military powers around them. The people looked to all kinds of false religions. The one true direction to which the people should have turned was being ignored. As God foretold, the inevitable happened. Disunited, corrupted, with no moral strength, the nation fell an easy victim to invading forces. It was carried off into captivity.

But the prophet never lost hope. He heard the Word of the Lord, calling to people to re-focus their attention: "Look to ME and be saved." A remnant would be left, cleansed and purified by suffering. And this remnant would re-start the nation's life.

In the disturbances of our own times, in our own country and worldwide, God says the same thing. "Look to ME and be saved." He is also asking again the question put to Isaiah, "Who will go for us?" If we could reply: "Here am I, send me." we would be doing the biggest possible work for our country and for the world. But this means disciplining ourselves, every day, to *make* time in which we offer ourselves without reserve to be a channel for the will of God to flow into His world for his saving work. It requires that we turn and 'look to' God, the I AM, as naturally as a plant turns to the sun.

Mobile God

"I have been moving from place to place (with a tent as MY dwelling)"
(2 Samuel 7.6 NIV)

This Saying is perhaps not as familiar as many which might be chosen, and yet it is one which leaps powerfully out of the page and speaks to our situation and world today every bit as profoundly as it did when it was first spoken some 3000 years ago. Much of what we call 'The Middle East' is today very similar to what it was at the time of King David. Now, as then, nomads are to be found living in tents made of animal skins, in the wilder places between the towns and cities. A city dwelling usually speaks of stability and permanence. There is some merit in considering God as the One who is unchanging, permanent and totally reliable. But this view could lead both to complacency and rigidity. A tent as a dwelling is provisional, mobile, and imper-manent. Until Solomon built the first temple, this more hazardous way of life spoke powerfully of God who could not be manipulated nor controlled by any human endeavour.

The context of this month's Saying is the Israelites' consoli-dation of their nation under David. The ark has been recovered and brought to Jerusalem, and it is a period of prosperity and peace (2 Samuel 6.17). In this time of relative security, David humbly confesses to Nathan the prophet his unease that the Ark of God is still in a tent while he, David, dwells in 'a palace of cedar.' Our Saying is part of God's reply which the prophet must pass on to David. In this message, God indicates that he must be in control of events — he will permit David's son, Solomon, to build a temple, but God's 'occupancy' is voluntary: he will *choose* to dwell there, but he will not dwell in any temple which David decides to build of his own accord.

For us, like David, it can be disturbing to find that we have a 'mobile' God, and we might find life more comfortable if we could pin God down a bit. We may, like David, try to restrict God by means of a building — thinking of the church as the place where we meet him. Or we may try to set limits to his activity by deciding in advance what sort of things he is or is not likely to do.

But God refuses to be bound by our petty restrictions. He remains the God of the tent, forever moving from place to place and meeting us in ways and situations in which we least expect him. He may be more disturbing than we might like, but also far more dynamic and life-enhancing. For there is always the *frisson* of possibility in every moment that our surprising God may be just around the corner.

Molten Metal

**"MY people shall be tried ... as gold is refined ... in the
furnace of affliction"**
(Isaiah 48.10 & Zechariah 13.9)

This is a 'hard' Saying. If we are not careful, we may find
ourselves avoiding such Sayings in contemplative prayer,
focussing mainly, perhaps solely, on words that are 'comfortable.'
If we do this, then we are in danger of ignoring a very large part
of biblical teaching in both Testaments which is concerned to
warn and to challenge.

The Church in the 20th century tended to react against the 'hell
fire and damnation' type of preaching which was said to charac-
terise Christian proclamation during the 19th century. This was
probably a healthy reaction, reinforced by the shock of trying to
come to terms with the hellish business of two global conflicts.
There is also the fact that the Church and Christian theology have
been shaking off the shackles of an outdated medieval simplistic
system of rewards and punishments tied to an almost
geographical understand of heaven and hell. The pendulum,
however, has swung the other way. We no longer want to 'put the
fear of God' into people; but we are often fearful of listening to
and proclaiming the prophetic utterances which should leave us
in no doubt about the wages of sin and the Divine judgement.

One result of this shying away from the prophetic challenge is
an almost universal bewilderment on the part of our civilization
with respect to an understanding of pain and suffering and
death. These things are held to be an affront to human life and
dignity. The contemplative experience should reveal to us, and
through us to others, that in fact they constitute part of the
inevitable growing pains of a humanity which is, under God,

maturing to perfection. We must, therefore, include in our contemplation from time to time, the harder Sayings which give us a glimpse into the divine purposes, and also help the Church to proclaim the Gospel in its fullness, rather than a watered-down version designed as little more than a pain-killer.

Before using this Saying in prayer, it will be helpful to look up the following references and their contexts: Psalm 12.6; Proverbs 17.3; Ezekiel 22.17-22; Malachi 3.1-3; 2 Esdras 16.73 [Apocrypha]; 1 Peter 1.6-8.

Mountain Climbing

"Come up to ME into the mount, and be there"
(Exodus 24.12 AV)

This 'Word' spoken to Moses is a peremptory call to those who
'have ears to hear' to approach the holiness of God. Like Moses
and the prophets, contemplatives are called to represent
humanity before the Lord — to acknowledge His awesome
holiness (Isaiah 6.1-8) — to receive the Word, as Moses received
the Commandments — to make known by proclamation that
same Word.

This call *upwards* is significantly repeated in various parts of
the New Testament. Jesus, led (or driven) by the Spirit, is called
from the place of his baptism (the river Jordan, 1200 feet below
sea level) *up* to the wilderness for the time of testing. Pilgrims
visiting that part of the Holy Land are shown 'the Mount of
Temptation.' Jesus himself delivers his famous sermon 'on the
Mount' to which his followers are called (Matthew 5.1). His
closest disciples follow him *up* the Mount of Transfiguration
(Luke 9.28); and from another 'mount' he is raised to glory at the
Ascension (Matthew 28.16). And the Seer of Revelation hears the
trumpet-voice summoning him, "Come *up* hither, and I will show
you things which must be hereafter" (Revelation 4.1).

When you climb a mountain, your horizon is widened. Our
response to the call to contemplation similarly enlarges our
spiritual vision, and we gain perspective. The Word which is
spoken to us, like the Commandments of old, gives us direction
and purpose. And through us (by way of intercession, and again
like the Commandments) the Word becomes our spiritual gift to
the world for its redemption.

But before anything useful can happen, or be done by us, or

through us, we are called, as the Saying reminds us, simply to 'be there.' Sometimes, that is the most difficult part, for we are so often keen to be 'getting on with *doing* something,' or perhaps frustrated because, by disability, age or infirmity, we are inhibited from doing very much. But the Lord says: "Come up into the mount, and be there." Our prime task is to obey, just to *be there*, and listen.

My True Beginning

"Before I formed you in the womb I knew you . . .walk in MY ways"
(Jeremiah 1.5 and 1 Kings 3.14 NRSV)

Conventional knowledge would say that your life begins on the day of your birth, or on the day of your conception. Traditional wisdom which is in touch with spiritual reality teaches that our true beginning is totally prior to our physical being, in the womb of the spirit and the mind of God.

This Saying makes a profound mystical statement. Not only does it link each one of us with the whole 'stuff' of the physical universe by referring to our formation in our mother's womb. It looks before, behind and beyond that event to the time when we were held within the spiritual womb of creation, and known by God alone.

The reluctant prophet saw himself as inadequate for the task to which he was called — he was young, vulnerable, pathetically weak in a hostile environment. He is reminded forcibly of his true worth in God's sight: precious, loved, and an integral part of the eternal plan which is the consummation of goodness, beauty and truth.

It seems important to attach to the saying from Jeremiah the final four words which God spoke to the young Solomon. For with the recognition of one's true value in God's eyes comes the command or compulsion to share the vision with others, so many of whom are blind to it, and blunder on their way through life from crisis to crisis. When we obey the command to walk in the ways of I AM we shall naturally come face to face with the real world of pain, suffering and sorrow. But with the command comes the promise, "I will lengthen your days" — not so much an extension of life, but an enlargement of opportunities to carry out the work of the Lord, whether in active ministry or in prayer and intercession.

If God knows us so intimately, then he is more aware than we are of our weaknesses and our strengths. When life becomes fraught as we struggle to 'walk in his ways,' we can hear the assurance which he gave to Jeremiah (verse 8): "I AM with you to deliver you."

New Life

**"Behold! I make all things new . . . I AM the resurrection &
the life"**
(Revelation 21.5 & John 11.25)

In some ways, the Passion of Christ according to Saint John is the most forcefully dramatic account of the four gospels. It has a particular sense of grim realism and an air of poignancy about it which seems to get under one's skin. Yet John's writings are, in other respects, often other-worldly and ethereal. Above all, they emphasise life, and the triumph of life over death. When you read John you get a sense of the earthly and heavenly being very close together, and this is his essential message for earthbound humanity. You are closer to heaven than you may think.

This composite Saying links together John's two books. The two parts of the Saying could be used in either order; or simply one of them could be used contemplatively on its own, while the other remains, as it were, mentally in the background of our prayer.

It is tempting to conclude that nothing changes essentially. In spite of all kinds of novelty in the modern world, the same troubles and disasters occur, and that, as one writer put it, human beings still commit "the oldest sins in the newest kinds of ways."

Against this, the Risen Christ declares his intention, ability, and will to re-new the face of creation. When I am feeling a bit jaded or stale, I sometimes like to tell myself that absolutely nobody in this world has yet lived tomorrow. The entire and entirely unknown future, hidden in God, has yet to be entered by human beings, like a virgin snowfield without a single footprint on it.

The Resurrection of Jesus is like the first exciting footprint in the snow. It speaks of real new-ness, not mere novelty, and is a clarion call for people of faith to rally round the banner of life, when so many in the world seem locked in a losing battle against dereliction and death.

This is a good Saying to use in intercession, especially for the terminally ill, the hospice movement, and all who work with the dying and bereaved, including undertakers. Remember anyone who is fearful of death.

New Year Resolution

"I AM the bright morning star"
(Revelation 22.16 RSV)

At the very end of the Bible's last book, The Revelation to John on Patmos, Jesus, the Risen Christ, the Eternal One, the Alpha and the Omega, appears to John for the last time, identifying himself as the 'bright morning star.' This star is for the Church, to guide it in the ways of God; and now also, in the era of the living Christ, for the whole world.

In the season of the Epiphany, we ponder the story of the Three Wise Men. Their journey to find the Christ is in many ways the pattern for our own spiritual journeys. They were guided by a wonderful star through dangers and over great distances to worship Jesus. Perhaps they were surprised to find the Lord of Lords in such humble circumstances. We, too, must expect sometimes to be dumbstruck as we encounter the living God, the source and goal of all our contemplation.

We sometimes talk about 'following our star,' meaning our destiny. And the New Year is a good time to resolve to follow Jesus Christ 'more nearly,' as the One who is our bright morning star. Epiphany is a season of light, revealing things long hidden; a season of illumination, inspiration for all we are and all that we do. And Christ is the star of the dawn, the daystar, still shining as a point of light in the luminous clear skies of morning at his Nativity.

Christ is the evening star as well; the one who lights our way in the darkness and perplexity of our complex modern lives.

There has been much speculation about the nature of the universe, including its age and whether or not it is still expanding. How exciting it is that scientists have discovered micro-ripples of energy pulsing through the whole universe as it lives and moves in the hand of the Creator. The stars are not dead lumps of matter, but ever-changing, always being renewed, yet constant.

As we use this Saying in our contemplation, let us consider Christ, the Risen One, the Light of the World, the spiritual Morning Star, the One who lights our darkness and our dawn — the One who is here to illuminate our path, even when the clouds of trouble and distress seem to hide Him from us.

Night and Day

"I form the light and create darkness"
(Isaiah 45.7 AV)

The full text of this Saying (some may wish to use it all in contemplative silence) goes like this: "I form the light and create darkness; I make peace and create evil; I the Lord do all these things." Modern translations tend to gloss over the starkness of this Saying. That's why I always like to keep the Authorised Version handy.

God the creator of evil? Surely not! But then where did evil come from? Did it sneak in on God's day off?! Are there two stalls, then, in the Grand Bazaar of Eternity, held by two equal and opposite powers? ("Hear O Israel: the Lord our God is the only God" . . . Deuteronomy 6.4). Well, then; how can the One Creator be both all-good and yet create evil?

When I ask myself this reasonable question I can almost hear St Paul replying: "Thou fool!" (1 Corinthians 15.36). Back to Scripture, then, and especially the scripture about creation. What's that apple doing there in the Garden of Eden? It stands for choice — our choice, my choice. Why give me choice, then, if the results are so disastrous? Because free-will cannot exist in the absence of choice. All right; why free-will? Because love cannot be perfected by enforcement *and* (says God) "I made you in *my* likeness. You are *my* apprentices, and I will never leave you nor forsake you till each one of you loves perfectly as I love."

Tall order! God created all things 'good' (Genesis 1). Jesus said: "You must be perfect as your heavenly Father is perfect" (Matthew 5.48). Two different words: 'good' . . . 'perfect.'

I sense that evil is not a direct creation, but lies between the 'good' of Genesis and the perfection (or completion) yet to come.

Evil is stale goodness. The Latins were right: *Corruptio optimi pessima* – the corruption of yesterday's goodness will be tomorrow's vice.

A final thought: what is evil in one may not yet be so in another. The river of life bends, so that two people, both properly in the same stream, may at times be facing opposite. Evil applies chiefly when we get stuck in the sedge at the bends. God deliver us from that evil, because it is a strong temptation.

One at a Time

"Every living soul belongs to me"
(Ezekiel 18.4 REB)

Ezekiel was an exile — one of the citizens of Judah who were carried off to Babylon in the first captivity, with king Jehoiachin (see Ezekiel 1). This implies that he was among the cream of the population, the aristocracy. Settled into exile by the banks of the river, or canal, Chebar, after five years he began to have visions and to prophesy, about 593 BC.

In his writing, all in the first person, he hears God calling him 'son of man,' and his perception of the Deity places God a great distance away, in awesome majesty, above and beyond the world of men, all-seeing, all-knowing, in fire and glory. Against this was shown, in stark contrast, the people's sin and the consequent inevitability of judgement. This was the theme of the prophet's early ministry. But one of the most characteristic of Ezekiel's themes is that of personal responsibility; that each individual must answer for himself to God and not claim to be the victim of heredity, or environment, or historical causation.

Here in chapter 18, we are shown the other side of the coin, a wonderful reassurance. Just as each individual is accountable to God, so God takes responsibility for each individual: "every living soul belongs to me." He may be distant, majestic, and awesome, yet he is there, building the relationship with the people and foreshadowing the new covenant that will be spoken of in chapter 36: "you shall be MY people and I shall be your God."

As we listen to this Word and let it sink into our hearts, we become increasingly aware of the mystery of God's nature. When we consider the teeming crowds of the world's population, the seething masses at a pop concert or a peace demonstration, or the millions whose lives are blighted by disease and starvation, it seems incredible that 'every living soul' belongs to the Lord.

Our concerns for intercession seem sometimes to become an endless list; but it is not so for God. We can use this Saying in confidence that there is no thing and no-one too small, nor any number too large, for his concern and care and blessing.

Open thou our lips

"I will give you a mouth and wisdom"
(Luke 21.15 RSV)

To be lost for words is a common experience. Jesus tells his followers that, when it comes to standing up for what they believe, for the Gospel, they will not be lost for words. Those who are in the habit of daily receiving in contemplation God's life-giving Word find that they are being provided with a divine vocabulary, grounded in God's wisdom. This stands us in good stead in those tricky situations when we may be lost for words, whether preachers or teachers of religion struggling to find how to 'put it across,' or anyone caught up in a situation where helpful words are needed to sort out a problem.

This Saying echoes strongly the Word of God to Moses in Exodus 4.12. Hesitant to be leader and God's spokesman, he hears the Lord saying to him, "I will be with your mouth, and teach you what you are to speak." Jeremiah felt the same reluctance and was told by God, "I put my words into your mouth" (1.8). As someone who has to prepare sermons, I am constantly recalling that Saying, both as a challenge as well as for encouragement.

A minister once told me that he had learnt a beautiful lesson about words and wisdom. As a young vicar, he went to visit an elderly widow who had recently been bereaved. As he was struggling to find the right things to say, there came a knock on the door, and a neighbour came in to offer his condolences. This man's wife had recently died, and the vicar listened spellbound as this neighbour expressed in simple terms, and with great effectiveness, all that the vicar had been trying to say for the previous half hour. He felt that God had not only given the neighbour 'a mouth and wisdom,' but that he, too, had received the same gift for future use.

Our contemporary world is chock full of words which pour out endlessly from the media. But it is a world which is lacking in wisdom which ultimately derives solely from the Word of God. It is therefore all the more vital that we are in tune with that Word so that it may be made available for others.

Overcoming Fear

"Do not be afraid; only have faith"
(Mark 5.36 NEB)

In September 2001 the world was caught up in a vortex of fear. What sometimes goes unrecognised is the fact that the apparent bravado of terrorist activity is a plausible screen masking a reservoir of dread. This is true of human aggression in general, and this is why, in sacred scriptures and especially in the Bible, the words 'Fear not' appear so frequently. These words are spoken, not only to an individual or a nation in Biblical times, but to all human beings today, and eternally. In the rising and falling of empires, in the passing of great leaders and wise philosophers, the Words of I AM remain like a rock amidst the swirling changes of space and time.

This Saying was initially spoken to a local religious leader named Jairus. He had begged Jesus' help because his daughter was at death's door. Jesus set off with him to his home, but a messenger stopped them with what must be the most fearsome message any parent could hear: "Your daughter is dead." Immediately, Jesus forestalled Jairus's reaction by saying, "Do not be afraid; only have faith."

Whenever we face moments of despair or horror, these words are for us. We may be as desperate and distraught as Jairus was. If so, we may have to do as Jairus did: we may have to fall on our knees and plead for help. Then we shall need to hear, over and over again, the Divine response: "Do not be afraid; only have faith."

Fear is like a dark cloud or thick fog, cutting us off from God as surely as a switch cuts off electric current. We have to turn from fear, and from every messenger of doom and gloom, to the

Word of I AM. Then his love, wisdom and power are able to flow into us, bringing his peace. "Only have faith." Faith that his Word is true; faith that whatever comes, he will carry us through it; faith that in the end, however terrible the present moment, everything will be alright. Faith comes as and when we learn to put ourselves completely in his hands. Faith is the concomitant of trust. "Trust in God always; trust also in me" (John 14.1 REB).

Peace as a Gift

"Peace I leave with you, my peace I give to you"
(John 14.27)

As the Lord makes clear in the words that follow this Saying, this peace is different. It is peace that is "*not* as the world gives." The world's peace is largely negative: an absence of conflict, a temporary oasis amid turmoil, a moment of rest in the midst of busy-ness. By its nature the world's peace is impermanent.

We are restless beings, if not physically, then mentally and emotionally. As one writer put it, it seems that videos play constantly through our minds even if our bodies are resting. Yet human beings also long for real peace, a quality described by the Hebrew word *shalom*. This was the familiar greeting in the Palestine of Jesus' day as it is in the Middle East today. It carries the meaning of a wish that health and well-being will be given to the one you greet. There is an echo of this in the English word *hallo*, deriving from the same source as the words 'health' and 'wholeness.'

People of good-will can, to some extent, share this peace with others. It is fortunately built into our nature. By nature, walking down the street, we tend not to annoy other people by getting in their way or tripping them up. With some notable exceptions in today's society, most of us prefer to get on with other people rather than to be contentious.

But sometimes you come across a person who possesses an inner peace that appears to be transcendent. This is the divine gift born of faith and loving trust in God. The French priest-philosopher-scientist, Pierre Teilhard de Chardin, worked as a stretcher-bearer during the mayhem of the trenches in the first World War. Many soldiers commented on the extraordinary peace-full-ness that he seemed to wear like a garment amid the carnage and chaos of that fearful conflict.

This is the parting gift of Jesus to his disciples, the real 'shalom,' the peace of God that passes all understanding. The more deeply we can let this Word sink down into our inner self, the more we shall be able to receive the spirit and life of God's true peace into our own lives, and be able to share it with others.

Planning for Life

"I know the plans I have for you"
(Jeremiah 29.11 NIV)

These words come from a letter written by Jeremiah, in Jerusalem, to the exiled Jewish people in Babylon. For over six hundred years the people had been living in the land which God promised them, and they had built their temple in the Holy City. Then, in the year 587 BCE disaster struck. The Babylonians invaded, Jerusalem was captured, and many of the citizens were carried off into exile. There they must have been in despair. How could they worship God in a strange land? (Psalm 137.4). How were they to carry on a normal life? Not only were their own plans frustrated; it seemed as though God's purposes had been frustrated too. They had been taken away from the place which he had prepared for them. Perhaps they felt that God had abandoned them. Certainly they felt that they were in the wrong place.

In this situation God speaks to them through the mouth of the holy prophet Jeremiah. He tells them that it is he, God himself, who has carried them into exile, and after 70 years he will bring them back. In the meantime they are to build houses, plant gardens, marry and have children, and seek the prosperity of the place where they are living. God's word is, "I know the plans I have for you, plans to prosper and not to harm you, plans to give you hope and a future." God is in control, he wills their good, and they are to trust him.

We make plans for our lives, and we like to be in control. Sometimes things seem to be going according to plan, but often we feel that our plans are frustrated, and we may feel that we are in the wrong place. We may think that our circumstances are so difficult that we can't carry on a normal life. Perhaps we have set out along a certain path, thinking it is God's will, and then it all goes wrong and we feel that God's plan has been frustrated as well as our own. Or we may feel that he doesn't care.

God speaks to us as he spoke to the exiles in Babylon. He is in control. He makes his plans in love, to prosper and not to harm us. Whatever happens to us, whatever mistakes we make, he can turn them to our good.

Pole Star

"I am the Lord, unchanging ... return to me, (and) I will return to you."
(Malachi 3.6-7 NEB)

You may find this sentence a bit too long to retain in the mind in contemplative silence. If so, then the first part will suffice on its own, although while reflecting on the Saying it is as well to consider both parts.

In the parable of the Prodigal Son, you will remember that when the son was on his way home, while he was still some way away, his father ran out to meet him. So the son is greeted and welcomed before he has completed his journey home, simply because his father, who stands here for God the Father, is unchanging and cannot cease to love (Luke 15.20).

The conditional "if you return..." is included in the text, but this should not be interpreted as God holding back a blessing until we do as we are told. Rather, it is a common-sense equation when you come to grasp its spiritual significance. When by an act of will we turn truly God-wards, this movement is matched by a new realisation that God is pouring out His Spirit upon us in an effusion of unchanging love. The more we proceed along the pilgrimage path of the spiritual life, the more we come to understand that God's initiative is paramount, and any good that we do is by way of our response to his prior activity. Mission work is no longer conceived as taking Christ to the unbelieving, but of knowing that Christ is there before us and sharing that knowledge with those with whom we engage.

We are told by Jesus, "continue in my love" (John 15.9). This is because we vacillate and are variable in our praying and striving to do God's will and to follow the example of Jesus

Christ. So for our soul's health we need constantly to *turn* or *return* (re-turn) to the "Father of the lights of heaven with whom is no variableness" (James 1.17. This whole chapter of James's epistle speaks volumes to our "natural" condition). So in our instability, "to whom can we turn" except to God — the one truly unchanging factor in all circumstances of change and decay. For he, indeed, has "the Word of eternal life" as Saint Peter discovered (John 6.68).

Pot Shot

**"Just as the clay in the hands of the potter, so are you
in MY hands"**
(Jeremiah 18.6 RSV)

God and Jeremiah are having a conversation. Or, to be more exact, as so often happened, God is speaking to the life and the divine calling of his much-loved prophet. Jeremiah did as God instructed him and describes the scene.

In the potter's house he saw the potter with the clay on the wheel but the pot he was making was marred or ruined in his hands (if you have ever tried pottery you will know how quickly the clay can become a wobbly mess on the wheel!). So the potter began to form it into another pot as seemed best to him. The clay wasn't discarded, but reshaped, and not only reshaped but given a new design, a new purpose. Moulded into another pot as seemed best to the potter.

The message of course related to a nation, God's chosen people. The people through their disobedience of God's law had become marred or ruined in his sight. As the visual aid of the potter shows, God would not disregard them but begin again to refashion them, bring a renewed hope and a reconciled relationship. Recreate them and the covenant relationship as seems best to God the potter.

What applies to a nation is relevant also for individual people, each one a child of God. In the Bible, especially the Old Testament, it is sometimes not possible to distinguish whether God's Word is being spoken to an individual or to the nation as a whole. So if you were to go to the potter's house, and place yourself on the potter's wheel, what changes would your creator make? What changes would you beg him make? The one thing you can be sure of is that you will not be discarded. Changed? Maybe. Challenged? Definitely! Because it is in the potter's house, in the hands of the potter, that re-creation happens, new purposes are given and relationships restored.

One of the early church fathers encouraged: "Offer the potter your heart, your life, your hopes, yours fears, and allow him to refashion you, remake you, let your clay be moist and workable lest you grow hard and lose the imprint of the potters fingers."

Mindful of our own needs for re-newal, we do well also to consider this Saying as one spoken to the society in which we live, giving us direction for our intercession.

Recycled Sin

"I will make the Valley of Achor a door of hope"
(Hosea 2. 15 RSV)

The story behind this verse comes from the book of Joshua, chapter seven. After the capture of Jericho, Achan sinned badly in this valley of Achor by coveting, stealing and concealing some precious objects from among the spoil the Israelites had decided to devote to God. He was found out by Joshua and punished severely. The valley was then named the Valley of Achor, meaning 'trouble.'

The verse itself is from the prophecy of Hosea. God had previously been complaining about the unfaithfulness of the Israelites to their covenant with him, but now he changes his tone and says that he will allure Israel into the desert and speak tenderly to her. He will restore her vineyards and make the valley of trouble a door of hope. The Valley of Achor was actually a route out of the desert into the heart of the land. Sometimes we feel that we are in a desert spiritually, and long to find a way to the heartland — a way to spiritual richness and lushness once again. God seems to be promising that here. We cannot find our way there on our own, but God will open that door for us, and surprisingly it is the very door that had been a trouble to us before. God not only forgives; he re-names troubles. He has a zero waste policy as far as human beings are concerned, somehow absorbing our sinfulness and bringing transformation.

I don't suffer from depression, thank God; but there are times when I feel like Eeyore in *Winnie the Pooh* — gloomy, edgy, dissatisfied with myself and the world. But when the clouds pass and I resume my customary cheerfulness, I just know that I have been tested for my own good, even if it didn't feel like it at the time.

God will not destroy the Valley of Achor, which was a valley of shame, guilt, sin and failure. Instead he is going to make it into a door of hope, into a place of new beginnings. Transformation happens when we turn all our life with its sins over to God. The best time for transformation to happen is contemplative prayer. We live in a world that is badly in need of transformation. Through prayer God can transform valleys of Achor into doors of hope.

Reliable Testimony

"You are (shall be) MY witnesses"
(Isaiah 43.12 and Acts 1.8)

To be effective, a witness (of a road accident, say) needs to have been near to the scene. Yet there is some virtue in the testimony of someone who, from a vantage point further away, is both less emotionally involved and may have a clearer perspective.

The witness to religious truth is, in a sense, called to fulfil both these roles. On the one hand, he or she must maintain, through prayer and study, that intimacy with the Lord whom they seek the follow ("Abide in ME" John 15.4). At the same time, their vision needs to be sufficiently broad to encompass both the glories of the created universe and also the hopes and fears and strivings of contemporary human society.

In the Old Testament context for this Saying, the Word came to the prophet in the unlikely setting of deprivation and exile. In spite of setbacks, the exiles are to be (are still to be) witnesses of "I AM," as verse ten makes clear. They must look beyond the narrow confines of current difficulties and regain the wider vision.

The New Testament echoes the Saying at the start of Luke's second book, the Acts of the Apostles, where the disciples of Jesus are given their commission. They have the added joy of becoming witnesses to the Word-made-flesh, the one who is dwelling among them. Their perspective must also broaden, beyond the confines of the Holy City of Jerusalem, "to the uttermost parts of the earth."

It is difficult to decide whether the words in this Saying constitute a promise or a command. Perhaps it is best to keep both meanings in mind. On the one hand, once you have been grasped by the love of God, you cannot but find some way of making that known. On the other hand, there is often the need to 'bide one's time' a bit, and wait for the appropriate occasion when, at some future date, you may be a more effective witness than at the present. In the case of the apostles, they had to await the descent of the Holy Spirit for empowerment to do the work that God had in mind for them.

Safe with God

"Because you love me, I will protect you, for you acknowledge My Name"
(Psalm 91.14 NIV adapted)

Long before the books in the Bible were put into writing, the stories and songs, poetry and history were handed down by word of mouth. There were harvest songs, vineyard songs, wedding songs, love songs, private songs of sorrow and suffering, songs of triumph, songs for a defeat. These songs were part of the heritage of every Israelite, and many of them are encapsulated in the Book of Psalms.

In Psalm 91 we have a noble song of faith and trust, full of fire and energy. Love and trust go together. "Because you love me..." One stage in our Christian pilgrimage is to allow God to love us and care for us. But another stage is to love him and trust him in return, offering to him our weak and disjointed and interrupted worship, praise and adoration.

We will all of us be aware at times that God really does seem to protect us. But at the same time we all know of situations, of people, who have a profound trust and love for God, but who still suffer, often in terrible ways.

The protection that God offers to us and in which we put our trust, is not necessarily a physical protection. Rather it is like a divine 'envelope' of healing and wholeness that surrounds the very depths of our being. It is here that our faith and trust really make a difference. Once you become aware of the inward and spiritual protective shield, you begin to realise that what Shakespeare called "the slings and arrows of outrageous fortune" may be a subordinate, rather than a dominant, factor in our lives.

I am sufficiently old-fashioned to be uneasy when young

people or strangers use my Christian name. One's personal name is a precious commodity and to use it implies a closer relationship than the merely casual. Similarly, careless use of the Divine Name is uncomfortable for those who are within the household of faith.

"Because you love me, I will protect you, for you acknowledge My Name." Notice how the love of God and the Divine Name are brought together. On 1st January the Church by tradition recalls the Naming of Christ as Jesus. As we honour him, we are hallowing the Name of God, whose truest Name is I AM (see Exodus 3.14-15).

Salt of the Earth

"You are salt to the world"
(Matthew 5.13 NEB)

Jesus is talking to the disciples, or to the crowds, or both. But as far as we are concerned he is talking to us. And it will help if we put the emphasis on the second word, "You *are* salt to the world." This gives the Saying a proper sense of immediacy. If you, whoever you are, believe in God, then you *are* salt to the world, i.e. your faith is important way beyond yourself.

One of the most dramatic natural features in the Holy Land is the Salt Sea, or Dead Sea. The surface water of what is really a lake is well over 1000 feet below sea level, and its salinity is about nine times the average of the world's oceans. At the southern end of the lake the salt deposits are many feet thick. The top layer is full of impurities. These days is it all put to good use, but in the first century the top layer was considered unfit except to throw out on the paths and trodden on. The purer salt was deeper down, and that was valuable and put to domestic use.

In biblical times, pure salt, like many other things from the world of nature (healthy trees, clean water, radiant light, pure gold etc.) became a religious symbol. Because pure salt was able to preserve food, it came to represent endurance. Pure salt was, and still is, used in Jewish worship. "You shall not omit the salt of the covenant with your God; with all your offerings you shall offer salt" (Leviticus 2.13 NRSV). So salt is a symbol of God's covenant with his people; that is to say, an agreement that is binding, one that is to be valued and which will endure and be preserved for generations to come.

In this respect, then, this rather surprising use of the symbol by Jesus must be intended to tell those of us whose faith is secure that we are to remain faithful for the sake of others whose faith may be less so, or non-existent. We are also to preserve our faithfulness by striving to be as Christ-like as possible.

We also know that, as seasoning, a little salt goes a long way. We are therefore not to be discouraged if we ourselves feel uncertain or weak, or small in numbers in the face of a sea of unfaith. The Church, after all, began with only twelve apostles.

Self Worth

"You are precious in MY eyes, and honoured, and
I love you"
(Isaiah 43.4)

This is a simple statement. It is its own context; for God is speaking the Word within us, not just in the Bible. God the Holy One is conveying the Divine attitude, and utter generosity of spirit, and the humility that is the Deity.

Precious? Despite our years of fumbling and half-hearted discipleship? Yes; we are of immense value to God. This is just the start. We soon hear that we are honoured. Honoured? Despite perpetuating dis-unity in the one true Body of Christ? Yes; the Holy-humble one respects us to the *nth* degree!

Are we sufficiently assured? The theoretical answer is "Yes of course": but typical of God I AM, even more is poured out towards us. We are loved!

Jesus made this clear to the crowds who listened to him, many of whom were under-valued by the officials of their day. The parables of the lost sheep (Matthew 18.12) and the lost coin (Luke 15.8), and the bidding to consider God's love for the least of his creatures, the lowly sparrow, are ample testimony of this truth (Matthew 10.31).

In addition to being precious to God, and honoured by God, God's totality, his gently being within ourselves, makes us alive, human, and is reassuring us of the Divine indwelling value, respect and love which are all in action perpetually towards us; the common lot of all of us by Divine Grace — that we may match that self-expression of the Holy One (verse 7), as it was portrayed in the written record by Jesus Christ.

These holy attitudes towards us, of value, honour and love, if we persevere in faith, will become ours too, bit by bit, so that we may hold the same attitudes towards ourselves to start with, i.e. Divine self-love, as 'commanded' by Christ Jesus (you shall love your neighbour as [you love] yourself). This is so that we may hold other people in the same value, honour and love, letting the glory work in us, and through us (verse 21), and desiring this fruition. All breathtakingly part of the new things announced in Isaiah 42.9. We are caught up in the drama of the self-manifestation of God, Epiphany, of glory, all the year round.

Shield and Reward

"I am your shield and your exceeding great reward"
(Genesis 15.1)

This Saying was first given to Abraham when he was subject to great testing, having to leave home and friends, and to face an unknown future. His experience is shared by refugees the world over, and others, such as prisoners of conscience who endure long jail sentences. It could be ours if we had to face accident, sickness or bereavement. It will be ours when we come to the time of our own physical death. At these moments the future is unknown and may seem to be frightening. Then is the time to recall that Abraham, as Saint Paul said, was justified by faith; and we are children of Abraham. There may be courage; but ultimately it is faith that will see us through.

God assures us that he is our "shield" so that our inner being cannot be harmed, even if physically, mentally, or emotionally we may be subjected to intense stress. In faith we can come to understand that difficulties and obstacles which confront us may be necessary. Because, without them, we have no need to reach out to receive the greater strength that comes to us from God. That strength may be immediate, that is, without a mediator. But often it is available to us via other people, family or friends, or those unknown who are praying for us.

So gradually we can become increasingly aware of God's unending and all-conquering love, and of that unique relationship that God has with each of us individually. That is an "exceeding great reward" of our faith.

At various points through life we are prompted by the Spirit within to give up old ways of thinking and acting that are no longer of real use, and to launch out into new ways, to be ready for new experiences. At such times, like Abraham, we are being challenged to leave the apparent security of the known path that we have trodden up to that moment, and to follow the unseen spiritual direction. If we do this in conformity with the will of God, then even when the going is rough the reward will be great; nothing less than the unimaginable and inexhaustible riches of the love of God, of the I AM who is himself our shield in troublesome times and our reward at the end.

Spirit and Life

"My words are Spirit and Life"
(John 6.63 RV)

In the Revised Version of the Bible (19th century) the Saying reads "The words that I have spoken unto you are spirit and life," but for contemplative purposes the abbreviated version will be more practicable without distorting the sense.

There is no doubt that the charismatic movement had an enlivening effect on the Church during the second half of the 20th century. It may be likened to the loosening of an over tight necktie on a first-aid patient: it let some air in! At the same time, the enthusiasms which were generated were sometimes excessive, even damaging, when a true sense of proportion and control was lost. This was bound to happen when there was a misunderstanding of the traditional teaching about the Holy Spirit. Certainly, in the Bible, the gift of God's Spirit brought about enthusiasm, but he should always be understood as the Spirit of truth.

Our perspective can be regained by deep reflection on the Word of God, and this key Saying corrects any distortions, while at the same time providing the backdrop for all contemplative praying where the Word is involved. We have a kind of equation which works both ways:

My Words = Spirit/Life

This implies that, if we are to understand the Words of God, we must be prepared not simply to take them at their face value or in a literal sense. They are to be understood spiritually if they are to become alive and meaningful. This was very important for making sense of what Jesus had just been saying about eating the flesh of the Son of Man and drinking his blood (verses 53-56).

Alternatively:

Spirit/Life = My Words

Which is to say, if you want to understand the meaning of Spirit and to lead a truly spirit-filled and authentic life, then you need to listen attentively to the Word of God.

The charismatic experience may be remarkable and heart-warming, but it is only shallow and temporary unless it brings with it a desire to open one's inner ear and listen in depth to the Word of God who is the "I AM." This means doggedly persevering in contemplative listening — hearing, receiving inwardly, and doing the Word regardless of what one feels like.

Springtime

"I will be an inner spring, always welling up for eternal life"
(John 4.14 NEB)

The words are slightly but legitimately adapted. Jesus talks with the Samaritan woman who came to draw water from the well which is situated today in the Palestinian town of Nablus. The water I will give, he says, will be an inner spring always welling up for eternal life. She misunderstands him as you can read in John 4.

In the Bible, the prophetic vision of God's glorious future includes an abundant supply of water (Ezekiel 47. Revelation 22). The spiritual symbol derives from the physical reality of the people who live in the countries surrounding the Mediterranean for whom water can become a very scarce commodity indeed. It is marvellous to see the ingenious systems and cisterns that have been used for water control and storage for thousands of years in these countries.

Water and Spirit are closely linked in our scriptural writings. Freely flowing water in abundance is a clear reminder of the abundant flow of God's Spirit in creation and in re-creation. On the other hand, spiritual dryness is a constant hazard in human affairs. This manifest lack of God can be an experience that comes upon us, over which we may appear to have little control; the desert experience of depression is a case in point. This is certainly a trial, a time of testing like any other illness or disability. With God's help combined with good doctoring and faithful friends we are able to surmount it, and turn the negative to positive good.

Alternatively, spiritual drought can easily occur when human beings seek their own ends to the detriment of other people; when our focus of attention is on the good things of this world with scant attention paid to God who provides them for sharing as well as for personal enjoyment. An affluent society is prone to this kind of dryness and will simply feed on itself and lose all sense of purpose and direction.

By contrast, the contemplative discipline of 'drinking in' the Word of God enables that Word to become a vast inner reservoir upon which to draw for all circumstances of living. That reservoir is nothing less than Christ himself, always bubbling up for Life.

Start Again

"I AM making all things new"
(Revelation 21.5)

Saint John's vision of a 'new heaven and a new earth' often forms part of the reading at a funeral service: "There shall be an end to death, and to mourning and crying and pain; for the old order has passed away . . . These words are already fulfilled. I AM the beginning and the end."

We come to God, thirsty for his love. "Like as the hart desireth the water brooks, even so does my soul long for thee, O God" (Psalm 42.1). Returning to the former text from Revelation, we continue to read: "A draught from the water-springs of life will be MY free gift to the thirsty." We take this Word into our minds, to believe and to understand it a little more deeply and realise that it is a Word of hope. We may live now with mourning and pain, but we have the promise that he will wipe every tear from our eyes. Renewal is part of God's truth, which is eternal.

This is a vision for the future, and yet the words "are already fulfilled." Jesus is risen and ascended, and has said "dwell in ME as I in you." Yet sometimes we seem to go on in the same old way. Is it really possible to make me new? How do we open ourselves to the renewal in these words? By opening, not simply our minds, but also our hearts to the Saying.

Life with God is full of new beginnings. In Him is the renewal, of cold hearts and dimmed faith and all-but-extinguished hope.

But warm feelings, however exalted, can easily evaporate. Therefore, we seek to allow the words to penetrate and energise our wills. The renewal of our will is an awesome task. Strong forces within us and from outside militate against it. So we turn back again to the Lord who makes *all* things new. And in intercession, we become aware once again that the love of God and of neighbour spiral round one another — an intertwining of spiritual growth.

Re-_new_-al: or, re-new-_all_ if you like. A prayer to God to take all of me, and make me new in every part, to be more fit for his service.

Strength in Weakness

"My grace is sufficient for you; my strength is made perfect in weakness"
(2 Corinthians 12.9)

Dennis lay on the bed below the window in the back room downstairs. He had lain there, in paralysis, for several years. He had been confirmed in his bed by the Bishop, and he received the Sacrament of Holy Communion every month thereafter until his death. Lots of people came to his funeral, strangers unknown to the family. This was because at some time or another they had paid Dennis a brief visit and, paradoxically, had taken away from him in inspiration far more than they felt they had been able to give by way of friendliness. He inspired others because he was himself in-spired, breathed-into by the Holy Spirit.

This Saying was given to Saint Paul in response to his plea to God to deliver him from a recurrent and incapacitating illness (2 Corinthians 12.7). Some think it may have been epilepsy, possibly short-sightedness or perhaps even cataracts. The Word may be addressed to us too, at any time that we are afflicted by some serious trouble or setback. We may pray: "Please free me from this nagging pain, this great grief, this crisis coming upon me, this insoluble problem." And just when we are at our weakest, and only then, is the grace and strength of God revealed. Someone once said: "When we feel that we have reached the end of our tether, we find that God is at the other end."

Saint Paul was called to learn the hard way that the weakness of the Cross of Jesus was paradoxically the most powerful force for the salvation the world and for sinful humanity. So Paul's sufferings, including that 'thorn in the flesh' about which he was so troubled, proved to be strong witnesses for the Gospel mission that he carried out so successfully.

If we try to live in our own strength alone, then we are doomed to failure, and are likely to involve other people in our failure. When we turn to receive the spirit and life of God's Word, then immediately a window is opened into our troubles, however bad they may seem, and an opportunity is given for the grace and strength of God to enter. And mysteriously, without our knowing, that grace and strength can flow through us and out to other people.

Success Story

"Though you fight ... you shall not succeed ... without me you can do nothing"
(Jeremiah 32.4 and John 15.5)

To make progress and to succeed are both natural and important human aspirations. Yet both beg the questions — "What is progress? What is success?" Each is a two-edged sword. Progress in technology has given us the motor-car. On the one hand it is a fabulous magic carpet, and on the other hand a severe pollutant. Success in business can bring increased wealth, but often at the expense of someone else's increased poverty.

Humankind is slow to learn that the only achievement worth having is progress towards God, and spiritual teachers are unanimous in their continual efforts to get this message across. Text after text in the Bible repeat the warning of this Saying in various words:

"Man born of a woman hath but a short time to live" (Psalm 103)

"All is vanity; what do people gain from all the toil?" (Ecclesiastes 1.2)

"The day of the Lord is near" (Joel 1.15)

"This very night your life is being demanded of you" Luke 12.20)

. . . and so on.

You could continue to stack up texts of doom, but that is the mark of a depressive nature. Such warnings are in place to encourage us not to give up the struggles of life. At the same time they invite us to relate all our strivings to God and his purposes.

The two-fold Saying may, at first sight, appear to be negative, with Jeremiah prophesying military failure and Jesus pointing out our weakness and our frailty. Yet each makes the positive statement that human failure is God's opportunity. Jeremiah writes at a time of national disaster; yet at the same time he carries out an action of energising hope by investing in a piece of land (see Jeremiah 32.9 ff.).

And Jesus implies in his words that we shall achieve all the success that we need by maintaining our close spiritual bond with him (John 15.4). We may wonder why, after years of our being aware of third world poverty and hunger, the problem is still there. The answer is that the modern world has in very large measure turned away from God. Reverse the trend of God-less-ness which is characterised by greed and selfishness, and God's promises will be made good with the rich sent empty away and the poor satisfied (Luke 1.53).

Telling the Truth

"You shall be witnesses unto me"
(Acts 1.8)

This is both a privilege and a tall order which Jesus in his risen Self passes on to us. What a pity the Jehovah's Witnesses have to some extent debased the currency of the word 'witness.' The call to be a witness can be interpreted in a variety of different ways. Clearly it is a call to mission, and in this respect we can see it being obeyed in devoted and self-less Christian service all over the world. But the Church's activity in mission is of little avail without the firm spiritual base of deep and reflective prayer. There are many elaborate and expensive evangelistic campaigns using sophisticated technology to reach millions of people. However, such witnessing (if that is what it is) can exalt the glory of human achievement without necessarily being to the praise and glory of God's Holy Name.

A reliable witness must be one who has, first of all, been *in the presence* — an eye-witness, and an ear-witness too. Attentive listening to the Word in contemplation will open up new ideas as to what it implies for each of us individually to be a witness. Consider, for example, the context of this Saying in the first chapter of the Acts of the Apostles. There is an ever-widening circle for the area of witnessing. "You shall be witnesses in Jerusalem, in Judea, in Samaria, and to the uttermost parts of the earth." In a church setting, 'Jerusalem' will stand for a local congregation, a gathering of faithful people who are witnesses of God's Word to one another in teaching, learning, and loving support. 'Judea' is the wider circle of those with whom we have regular contact through family, friends, or at the workplace. Some are called to witness to God's love and truth in 'Samaria,' where there may be hostility and resistance. And today, the 'uttermost parts' are not so 'uttermost.' Might you be called to be a witness for God when you go abroad for work or for pleasure? Or on the Internet?

Consider also that the Greek word for 'to witness' is *martureo* from which we drive our word 'martyr'. Being a witness, whether in active evangelism, or in the field of spiritual mission (which is prayer) is no easy option. But we may be assured that our *spiritual mission* of intercession, will be able to go forth 'to the uttermost part of the earth,' and it will not require a satellite to help it along!

The Best

"I am ... God; walk before me, and be perfect"
(Genesis 17.1 NRSV)

These words to Abraham find an echo in the Gospels: "Be ye
therefore perfect, even as your Father which is in heaven, is
perfect" (Matthew 5.48). This reminds us that the words are
eternally spoken, and therefore we need to hear them as spoken
to us. And would we rather not hear them? They might bring us
near to despair, when we consider our many personal imperfec-
tions. But think again, and think more widely, more creatively,
and more imaginatively. Traditional spiritual teaching maintains
that God's creation, in its wholeness and its one-ness, is perfect in
spiritual terms. That part of the creation which we inhabit is in
the course of returning to that primal perfection. The garden of
Eden, therefore, is not in the past, but somewhere in God's future.
And Saint John's vision at the conclusion of the Bible's last book
reinforces this teaching with great emphasis.

As we plod on and on in our journey through this world,
faithfully listening to God's Word, we begin to realise the true self
in us, the perfected self which is part of the Supreme and perfect
Self — the One who says of Himself, I AM. John sums it up in his
first letter (1 John 1.3): "We are God's children now; what we will
be has not yet been revealed. What we do know is this: when he
is revealed, we will be like him." That is the true goal, to be like
him. We are to reflect here on Earth something of the glory of
God for which he has created us.

This, then, is why we continually strive for high moral
standards. We don't do it because 'the Bible says so.' Put it the
other way round. The Bible says so, because it is our joy and
calling constantly to aim for perfection. The only failure in this is

to give up trying.

The Coptic Pope Shenouda III, talking of perfection, wisely put it this way: "Think of a child at Grade 4 in school. She paints a picture. It looks peculiar to us; out of proportion, no perspective. But for the child, at that Grade, it is the best she can do; it is literally perfect. So it is for us, in our human endeavours, when we do our best, and don't give up trying."

The Goodness Factor

"Cease to do evil; learn to do good . . . your sins are forgiven"
(Isaiah 1.16-17 and Luke 5.20)

There is a strong strand of teaching in the Bible that connects misfortune with sin. In some instances, it can be both crude and cruel to make such a direct connection — the suffering of the innocent is a case in point. The teaching is strongest in the Old Testament, where it is robustly challenged by the book of Job. It is challenged again by Jesus, both in his association with sinners and in his teaching (e.g. concerning the tower of Siloam in Luke 13.4).

The relationship between human sin and misfortune, whether sickness or some other disaster, is clearly an extremely subtle one, and it cannot be ignored. This composite Saying will give us a contemplative background as we wrestle with and mull over the problem of suffering.

The Word of God through Isaiah has a sense of continuity about it. It is as if God is not content simply to shout, "Don't do this — do that." His Word here is more suggestive and reflective, as if he were saying "Strive continually to direct yourself from sinfulness and at the same time school yourself in thinking and behaving positively in the direction of goodness and love." (The Hebrew word for 'cease' has overtones of 'being flabby, idle, ineffectual.' So one's attitude towards sin is to see it as something essentially weak and useless, not worth the candle).

Then comes Jesus, boldly pronouncing God's forgiveness to a paralysed man — something the patient needed but didn't ask for. The hidden subtlety of the sin/sickness connection is stated, but at the same time the flow of God's healing love is not impeded, and the paralytic walks home. This brings about a confrontation between Jesus and the authorities. Consider the vexatious reactions of those who have abused their bodies with drugs or alcohol when they are faced with a refusal of medical treatment.

When we have received this Word in mind and heart, and secured it as a watchword for daily life, we can use it in careful intercession for the sick, but particularly for wrong-doers and for those who are morally deviant or numb. For it is only when they realise a sense of sin that they will be enabled to "turn from their wickedness and live" (Book of Common Prayer).

The Greatest

"All is mine . . . I have chosen you"
(Psalm 50.12 and John 15.16)

It is sometimes both illuminating and helpful to place together two Sayings from different parts of the Bible when there is a clear link between them. The link in this instance is obvious when you look at Deuteronomy 10. 14-15. "Although heaven and the heaven of heavens belong to the Lord your God, the earth with all that is in it, yet the Lord set his heart on your ancestors alone and chose you their descendents after them, out of all the peoples, as it is today." A similar Word from the Lord is to be found in Exodus 19. 5-6.

There has always been a tendency in religion to adopt a dualistic way of thinking. Broadly speaking, this means thinking of creation as consisting of two parts, the God part which is spiritual and all-good, and the other part which is in some way against God; physical and material rather than spiritual, or an area of badness and evil beyond God's control which some people may think of as the domain of the devil.

Dualism may be sometimes useful as a kind of working hypothesis when we are coping with the shadow-side of creation and of ourselves. But the Biblical understanding of God is that He is sovereign Lord of all, and "in his hands are *all* the corners of the earth" (Psalm 95). In some mysterious way, which we find difficult to comprehend, all things, all creation, the good, the bad and the ugly, are held by God, from the merest sub-atomic particle to the vast extent of the universes. Nothing is outside or beyond the Divine supremacy of the One who is all-love, all-wisdom and all-power.

Moreover, just as mysterious is the assertion that we, people of faith, are called by the Supreme Sovereign to affirm this truth, and to make it known. This is as important for the human race and its future as it is for the environment. The whole of Scripture makes it very clear that God's way is to select or choose certain people to cooperate with Him in the work of completing and perfecting the created order. The chosen people are not just one race, but all sincere believers in God and his supremacy, called to take part in the process of redemption.

The Power of Love

**"Behold! I have given you authority . . . nothing shall
hurt you"**
(Luke 10.19 RSV)

The Greek word for 'authority' is *exousia*, which means literally
'out of one's own being' — and so, that which emanates from the
individual person to affect another person. God has given us
authority, which is not the power to bear down on other people
(bullying), but the gracious gift of using his Love-Wisdom-Power
to influence others for their good and to be influenced by them
for our own well-being. And this grace of true authority, love-
motivated, is a gift of creation, a natural human endowment.
Sadly, it is often misunderstood, mis-used and distorted by
selfishness.

As if to draw us constantly back to its true meaning, the Lord
prefaces this Saying with the word "Behold!" Originally this
means, not a mere passing glance, but "Take careful note —
ponder these words and go on pondering!" The words are not
therefore to be taken at their surface value, but are to be built into
our thinking, our feelings, and our activity for continual
reference both in our prayer-time, and as we go about our daily
business.

"Nothing shall hurt you." The Saying was first used in the
context of the sharing of the good and challenging news of the
coming of the kingdom of God (see Luke 10. 1-9 and 17-20).
Those who are called to share these spiritual riches are
vulnerable — they can be hurt, frequently were in Christian
history, and still are. Some people can be the object of a curse of
an enemy, or you might simply be having a run of misfortunes so
that odds appear to be stacked against you: the rather vague yet

familiar feeling of being 'got-at.'

But provided that, in the exercise of our God-given 'authority' (ex-ousia), we are clearly focussed on the Love-Wisdom-Power of I AM, then whatever comes back to us from others, even if it be a distorted and mal-intentioned authority bearing down upon us, it will not be able to cause us real harm or hurt (see Psalm 91). In fact, our inner store of wholeness will flow more freely as we become more sensitive in intercession to the needs of others, including the deeper spiritual needs of those who are outwardly malevolent.

The Right Balance

"Be still and know that I am God"
(Psalm 46.10)

This is one of the key quotations from the Bible that is known, revered, re-visited and lovingly remembered by countless numbers of those who are drawn to meditation and contemplative prayer. Psalm 46 is a song celebrating victory and peace. It is a call to those who seek to settle their differences in battle to de-commission their weapons and to remember God who alone wields supreme power from which all human powers derive.

Our Western civilization, including its religion, since the Reformation and especially during the past 200 years, has been characterised by activity. To be found 'doing nothing' brings a sense of guilt to many people. Even when we have come to terms with that and have decided to enter into stillness and quiet, this is by no means the end of the struggle. There can always be that nagging voice which says, "How can you be wasting time in this non-relevant way?"

In fact, however, this is the most relevant thing that we can do. If God is the Source of all, including all activity, then to know him is to engage in the most intense activity that is possible. And to listen at depth to the Word of God, if it is sometimes (indeed often) comforting, it is or should also be challenging us at some level of our daily lives.

Activity, even with good intentions, can be misplaced. It was once said of a bustling Christian lady that she was forever doing good for other people, and you could tell who the other people were by their hunted expressions! At the other extreme, to practise stillness and quiet for its own sake, even in prayer, can lead to quietism and self-centredness. Knowing God is knowing how to achieve the right balance.

Our best model, as always, is Jesus. The Gospels record how he withdrew and went away by himself for essential re-freshment, re-ordering, re-focussing in the closer presence of God in contemplative prayer. He would then return to engage once more with the crowds to share God's Word with them and minister God's healing. And in the final battle, he returned from the prayer of Gethsemane with courage to engage the powers that thought they should put an end to him.

The Winner

**"In me you have peace; (in the world you have tribulation
but) ... I have overcome the world"**
(John 16.33 RSV)

Words of strength and comfort from the Divine Source of all
power and peace. By being united with God, resting in him, we
can be in the world but not of the world. He offers us his peace,
which passes all understanding and which the world cannot give
(John 14.27). This peace is to be found within ourselves, where he
leads us to dwell with him in the deep centre of being. It is a
peace that we can draw on in our daily lives even when
surrounded by un-peace. For in all circumstances God knows
exactly what is happening to us and around us and how we feel
about it.

Having made himself vulnerable in the world in Jesus, God
now pours out himself (his divine Self) unceasingly in his total
self-giving of redeeming love for his creation.

Perhaps we are fortunate in that our daily lives may seem
relatively tranquil. Yet we cannot but be aware of the constant
'un-peace' and tribulations of God's people. We may find it
among our neighbours, in our families, and among our fellow-
worshippers. We certainly see it in economic problems and difficulties, in terrorist attacks, in injustice and oppression, and
among the deprived peoples of God's world. All these matters are
calls on our time for the deep and essential task of intercession.
We continue to do this spiritual work in the knowledge that God
in Christ has overcome the world. The world, ultimately, did not,
and could not destroy him. Neither can the world powers
overturn the divine purpose, which is to sum up all things in
love. So we align ourselves in prayer with God's perfect goodness

which is constantly engaged against evil and the forces of darkness.

Persevering in this course, we shall not ourselves be overwhelmed either by the world's sorrows or our own, nor by the magnitude of the task of prayer. In contemplation we shall receive the gift of inner peace and allow that peace to overflow and help to irrigate those places which are parched for the lack of God's saving Word and works.

A practical tip. As you watch or listen to the news, or when you read your paper, bring these words into focus in your mind: *In me you have peace...I have overcome the world.*

Timepiece

"MY hour has not yet come"
(John 2.4 REB)

This word is meant for all of us. When it is said to Mary at the wedding at Cana in Galilee, it is part of a story which sounds as though the Lord is rebuking her. Those who hear the Word of God and keep it become the Lord's mother, sister and brother. When we listen to, and receive, the Word with our mind, our heart and our will, we share with Mary and with one another the wonder of the Word made flesh. The wonder is that the Lord God, the maker of matter and time and space, who yet dwells beyond them all, chooses none the less to become one with all the time in the world, all the space, and with all that is, seen and unseen.

The bits and pieces of the universe all have their time element built in to them. "Every dog has its day." These moments are God given. Each moment is a bit of time and of space that comes in God's good time. "Out of eternity each day is born" as the hymn says. It is in this context of time that we hear this Word to wait upon God, and to wait upon the future in God. We are waiting for the 'hour' of the Son of Man.

The Coptic Pope Shenouda III was once asked: "How in my busy life do I find time for God?" After a moment's thought he responded: "You don't find time for God: you enjoy time with God." I like that.

There's a book by Toffler called *Future Shock*. It gives a dramatic doomsday scenario of what the world's future holds, based on a review of current global policies. It is one of many warnings which should alert us to change our ways. Yet in the life of the spirit, we know that the future is entirely in God's hands.

He cannot fail and his glory will be revealed in His time, not ours.

The One whose "hour is not yet come" calls us to wait in trust. We have no need of fortune-tellers, because the hours, days, months, and years to come are all in the hand of the Lord of time. "It is not for you to know the times or periods that the Father has set by his own authority" (Acts 1.7). We wait upon Him and thus renew our strength.

True Joy

"These things have I spoken unto you, that MY Joy might remain in you, and that your joy might be full" *
(John 15.11 AV)

In their sometimes frenetic pursuit after pleasure (often called 'Fun') large numbers of people are missing out on that deep sense of satisfaction and well-being which is implied by the word 'joy' as it is used here and elsewhere in the Bible. How can you truly 'en-*joy* yourself' if you never get beyond the pleasures which must inevitably pass away? True joy can be experienced even under adverse circumstances. At the end of his gospel, Luke notes significantly that the disciples of Jesus returned to Jerusalem "in great joy" immediately following the Ascension of the Lord (Luke 24.52) — a time of departure when sadness and sorrow might have been expected.

Ponder these words from Dietrich Bonhoeffer who suffered martyrdom at the hands of the Nazi regime:

> Joy belongs, not only to those who have been called home (the departed), but also to the living, and no one shall take it from us. We are one with them in this joy, but never in sorrow. How shall we be able to help those who have become joyless and fearful unless we ourselves are supported by courage and joy?
>
> I don't mean by this something fabricated, compelled, but something given, free. Joy dwells with God; it descends from him and seizes spirit, soul, and body, and where this joy has grasped a man it grows greater, carries him away, opens

---

* In modern versions the word *full* is usually translated *complete* which perhaps makes better sense.

closed doors. There is a joy (i.e. pleasure, or fun) which knows nothing of sorrow, need, and anxiety of the heart; it has no duration, and it can only drug one for the moment.

The Joy of God has been through the poverty of the crib and the distress of the cross; therefore it is insuperable, irrefutable. It does not deny the distress where it is, but finds God in the midst of it, indeed precisely there; it does not contest the most grievous sin, but finds forgiveness in just this way; it looks death in the face, yet finds life in death itself.

True Love

"Do you love ME more than these?"
(John 21.15 NRSV)

Note. Some people are hesitant about using a question for contemplative prayer. You could use instead John 13.34, "Love . . . as I have loved you". The commentary is relevant in either case. But if you use the second option, have this question also in mind.

There are many texts in the New Testament where Jesus unpacks what it means and involves to obey the first great commandment: "You shall love the Lord your God with all your heart, and with all your soul, and with all your mind." (Matthew 22.37).

The text we are considering involves surrendering our relationships unreservedly to God so that they become an integral part in our total commitment to God. What we are considering is *surrendered* relationships, released of their possessive elements. We do not reject or divorce ourselves from those we love, but love them in a new way in Christ.

This Saying, which was addressed to Peter, did not mean that he had to leave his fellow disciples with whom he had been ever since they chose to follow Jesus (and probably in business with them for a good many years before that). Obviously not; for they were key people in the implementation of Jesus' instruction to Peter to "feed my sheep." When Jesus said "more than these," he was asking for a 'surrendered' relationship with these disciples. This surrendered relationship is stated more emphatically in Luke 14.26: "Whoever comes to me and does not hate father and mother, wife and children, brothers and sisters, yes and even life itself, cannot be my disciple." This may sound strong stuff, but how often have we heard of people having to struggle with over-possessive relationships within the family bordering on neurosis, which impair not only their own growth but also the growth of those they love.

When David Watson was facing terminal illness he felt God prompting him to clench his fist. Then he was to open his hand one finger at a time, starting with the little finger. Each finger represented an aspect of his life that he was loath to part with. When he came to the forefinger, this represented his wife and children. Then finally he opened his thumb — his own life, now ending, that God had given him; and thus he presented a completely open hand for God to do whatever he willed.

(See also Genesis 22.2; Matthew 12.46-50; John 19.26-27)

True Vine

"I AM the true vine . . . you are the branches"
(John 15. 1 and 5 REB)

For a moment, let us join the disciples of Jesus in the Upper Room on Maundy Thursday and feel the tension and the urgency of the moment. 'The way' that the Lord had spoken about was a road leading through his full humanity towards his full mortality so that we might share his full divinity. The cost would be tremendous.

Now we leave the house and make our way to the city gates. The Passover moon is shining bright and full. As we look up to our left, we see Herod's magnificent Temple, one of the wonders of the ancient world. Jewish law forbade the adornment of sculpture and carving, with the exception of one of the ancient symbols of the Chosen People; the vine. The vine is unique among the trees. Its wood, fibrous and tough, is of little use, except for one purpose. It produces the richest, sweetest fruit of any tree that grows. The vine gives itself wholly to serve. The carving is gilded, glinting in the moonlight; and as he passes it Jesus says: "I AM the vine, and my Father is the grower, and you are the branches and will bear fruit that will last. Abide in me and I in you." So this oneness with the Father through the Son is a continuous movement of grace, as the sap in the branches can flow only so long as the branches stay on the vine stock — the same, obviously, with all plants.

This flow of the sap of love is all for one purpose (verse 11); so that 'MY' joy, the joy of 'I AM,' not our own personal self-contentment, will flow in and beyond us. In scripture, 'joy' is a word to do with action and response to grace, not just the so-called 'feel-good factor.' The action and response is towards the

Lord, the energy that we use and the choices that we make in response to faith. It is God's joy, the 'joy in heaven' (Luke 15.7), a joy to be shared (Deuteronomy 16.11).

To put a seal on all that Jesus has said, the True Vine must now be crushed, and the blood must flow for the healing of the nations.

Trust in His Word

"Don't be afraid. Only believe"
(Mark 5.36 GNB)

There must be few, if any, people who have never experienced fear. Fear is a useful stimulus to caution and action. We do not go into a lion's cage, and when a fire alarm sounds we quickly vacate the building. So fear is an essential survival mechanism; but it can often be a hindrance. Instead of urging us to sensible behaviour it can make us tense and agitated so that we can't think straight. It is that harmful fear that Jesus came to banish.

Jesus said, "Don't be afraid, only believe," to Jairus, the leading layman in a local synagogue. Jairus was dreadfully worried about his twelve-year-old daughter who was gravely ill and had begged Jesus to come and heal her. On the way to the house some people came from there with the heartless message that there is no reason to trouble the Lord further as the girl is already dead. If Jairus had been afraid before, his fear was now doubled and of that paralysing kind which makes us sink in despair. Jesus' words to Jairus are a powerful weapon against that kind of fear. They bring life and hope to the deadened soul. Jairus, as well as his daughter, was given new life through the words of Christ.

Only believe. We, like Jairus, can be released from the bondage of fear by turning our attention outwards, away from ourselves, towards the source of all being, love and goodness. Contemplative prayer is a very pure form of faith. As we become still, physically and mentally, we start to move into a state of being where we are no longer relying on our own resources for existence. We are no longer striving to achieve something or to improve ourselves intellectually or morally. Instead, we are simply relying on God alone, the Holy One who is both beyond and within. So try to remember to begin contemplation with a brief relaxing exercise in order to allow the tension of fear or anxiety to subside. 'Believing' is being open to God's power. We believe when we allow his voice to penetrate the depths of our being. These words of Jesus themselves produce faith as we listen to them in contemplative silence.

Untold Wealth

"I will give you . . . riches stored in secret places"
(Isaiah 45.3 NIV)

We thought we knew York well; we'd been there so often. But Simon Jenkins' book, *England's Thousand Best Churches,* directed us down a little lane, west of the river, to the hidden gem of All Saints Church, North Street. Here we found riches of which we'd been completely unaware; a medieval church with original stained glass, a hammerbeam roof, a roodscreen, and, primarily, an atmosphere of prayer and holiness. It was like finding the church of St Magnus the Martyr amongst the soulless blocks of the city of London. Such churches are symbols of God's riches, stored for us in secret places.

This verse from Isaiah, pledging hidden riches, was written at the end of the exile, a time of homecoming. God assures his people, not just of a new home, but of one which is thrilling beyond all expectation, where treasures are waiting to be discovered.

In contemplation we can ask God to show us something of the riches he has stored for us. He who created our vast universe, who turned water to wine in lavish profusion, has an infinity of treasure stored up which, if we are patient, he will reveal to us. Who, for example, would have thought of looking for the riches of the Incarnation, Emmanuel, God-with-us, in the back yard of a pub in Bethlehem where animals were stabled? God's wealth concealed in poverty and ordinariness.

But patience is the key. These treasures are not wide open to the world. They are in secret places, and we need to make time if we are to discover them. A temptation in contemplative prayer is to hurry, to expect too much too quickly. An archaeological dig does not reveal its artefacts as the first sod is turned; a code is not cracked without effort. We need to wait, our minds free, alert and uncluttered, until God shows us His hiding places.

Besides waiting, there is remembering. 'Count your blessings,' the saying goes. When we dwell on the riches we have already been granted, and recognize all God has provided for us, we are filled with wonder. We are not worthy, and yet we have received unsearchable riches, pouring forth as light from the sun.

Up you get!

"I say unto thee, arise"
(Mark 5.41 AV)

It is best to prepare to use this Saying in contemplation by reading the whole of Chapter 5 of Mark's gospel. People who first read this knew about the resurrection of Jesus. Other material about Jesus had been written down by Paul. Mark, in his account of the life of Jesus, includes parables, healings and miracles. His is a serious attempt to explain the importance of the actions of Jesus to whom his Father had said: "With you I am well pleased."

Mark was writing about a struggle. The evil one was wanting to destroy life and was seeking the co-operation of people to achieve it. The cure of a woman which precedes the 'return to life' of the girl shows that Jesus will overcome evil and new life will be available (v. 25-34).

Both these occasions of healing are a response to need. Jesus recognised that, for example, the father had two possible responses — fear, or faith (cf. Mark 5.36). There will always be instances of chaos in human nature. In the community there is always someone in great need. Jesus, in responding to adult and to child, shows us a response to faith will come. Jesus affirmed the words of God, "I AM the Lord who heals you" (Exodus 15.26).

There are moments of darkness in a community's experience as well as in the experience of individuals. The way Mark wrote his gospel assumes these will continue even after the 'Kingdom of God' has been established. Out of the parables and healings and miracles comes the message that evil can be overcome. That new life is available. A turning in need to Christ receives the command: "I say unto thee, arise . . . get up."*

This is a message to offer for a new millennium; the message of resurrection, of life renewed. The church may sometimes appear weak and disabled, even bewildered about how to offer the Good News. The way of the One who came into the world was to get alongside its sadness and tragedy and to confront it. Mark was convinced that the story he was telling, although seemingly negative (a cruel death), was indeed and in fact a message of healing and hope.

-----

* "*Talitha cumi* is Aramaic meaning, 'Up you get, lassie!' It is what any Galilean mother might say to her daughter in the morning." (Ian Cowie. *Jesus' Healing Works and Ours.* Wild Goose Publications 2000)

V for Victory

"I will uphold you with my victorious right hand"
(Isaiah 41.10 RSV)

This verse from the prophet of the exile is a mind-blowing tonic, especially to anyone near the edge of despair. We might link it with the Word heard by Jeremiah, "I will satisfy the weary soul" (31.25). So the soul can, after all, relax and wait, "in quietness and confidence."

Our Saying is addressed to 'the servant' Israel (verse 8) and Jacob, who are one and the same person, or entity. Israel is the one who wrestles with God, signifying that he still has many problems to tackle. Jacob (deceiver) is the one who usurps what is another's, especially status or inheritance.

These incomplete characters are, according to this Word, the servant of God. But they are also, astonishingly, God's chosen. The right hand always symbolises the consciousness in life — here the conscious choice of God with regard to us, and the infallibility of that choice, based on the All-love, All-Wisdom and All-Power that is I AM, the Lord of All. This choice of us is symbolised also, as a reinforcement of the truth of the fact that God *can not* separate from us (verse 13), being held on our conscious side, i.e. that our consciousness of Our Lord I AM is *for ever* supported by the Divine All-Knowing of each of us.

So, away with despair! Our faith is given re-assurance that as our enemies are overcome so "The whole world's hatred, broken by our loving, shall bow to love, thine everlasting name" (4th century Greek hymn). You and I, going about our daily lives with varying degrees of enthusiasm are actually held in the All-consciousness of God, who in that vivid symbol goes through each of our trials with us. He upholds us in them and leads us through.

In this pilgrimage, we may (probably we shall) be wounded. But we can offer these wounds in our prayer. The prayer of Eucharist, when priest and people re-call the suffering, death and final triumph of Christ, is particularly significant. Individually and corporately upheld by the All-power of God-in-Christ, we are one with the whole of creation, finding our way back into God.

Water-spring of Life

"If any one is thirsty, let him come to Me"
(John 7.37 REB)

Jesus called out these words to the crowds in the temple, who were attending the Festival of the Tabernacles. This, one of the most important Jewish festivals, reminds those worshipping of the time that the nation of Israel spent in the desert, a reminder in ritual of the wanderings following release from slavery. Much of that time was spent in an arid landscape, with water in short supply.

Jesus called out these words with the immediate background of one special ritual — gathering branches with which to build the tabernacles, or temporary booths. And in that ritual, water was collected in a golden pitcher from the pool of Siloam. In this sacred setting of Jewish historical tradition, special and full of symbolism, Christ calls: "Come to Me — and drink."

In effect, Jesus is saying: "You are praising and thanking God for the water which quenches your physical thirst; but come to Me, if you want water which will slake the thirst of your souls."

At this moment, Christ turns men's thoughts to God, and to things Eternal. This was exquisite timing, dramatic, drawing attention to His every word, his very Word. And, like the woman at the well in chapter 4, as with the wedding at Cana in chapter 3, and the washing of the disciples' feet in chapter 13, Christ uses the analogy and example of water to illustrate the Way. In this symbolism will be found purity, cleanliness, being washed clean, humility, receiving the spirit — and the never-ending love and grace which God gives to his people.

The expression 'living water' (John 4.10) equates, in traditional biblical language, with clear, running water, full of oxygen bubbles — literally *water of life*. Small wonder, then, that water is used by Jesus as a way of expressing that which, through him, is available to all. Water is the vital commodity essential to sustain life. Water can make deserts flourish and blossom, plants to grow and to bear fruit. Water rescues and revives plants dying of thirst.

How much more will 'Living Water' achieve for men and women who are flagging, dry, isolated in an arid life, and out of touch with things eternal and spiritual? As people of faith, we may be aware of the 'Living Water,' of what it can do, and has done for mankind. We may have clear evidence that it can change and enrich the lives of men and women.

But we must also *be* the evidence, so that, in the way in which *we* live, others will approach Christ for a drink of that reviving, nourishing, sustaining water. We are to be the examples.

When Jesus calls: "Come, drink" — the invitation is now, and for ever.

Who's in charge?

"I will give authority . . . even as I also received authority from my Father"
(Revelation 2. 26-7 NRSV. See also Matthew 28.18)

The word 'authority' may prompt mixed feelings these days. There are plenty of people in positions of authority who abuse it. Perhaps authority is a quality that we feel that we neither have, nor particularly want. However, as a spiritual gift, true authority is something that ordinary people may receive from God, and treasure. So let us look at the people to whom this Word was spoken, through Saint John.

In the letter to the churches, John was writing to fellow Christians who lived in the western part of modern Turkey. This portion of the letter was written to Thyatira. Very little is known about this particular town, but what little we do know is interesting. It was small and relatively unimportant, but inscriptions have been found there which mention guilds of workers in wool and linen, tanners, potters, bakers, and metal workers. The picture emerges of an industrious community, contributing in essential but relatively lowly ways to the welfare of their society. It is not the sort of place or people that one would equate with notions of prestige or political status.

Nevertheless, it was to members of the small Christian congregation in Thyatira that 'authority' was promised as a gift.

Why were they singled out? Perhaps for the very reasons for which they were being commended. Nothing very great in the eyes of the world at large, but immensely precious to the Lord. Faith, love, service. Those ordinary men and women, and we too, are bidden to hold on to these values. More than that, we are bidden to persist in patient endurance, despite all the setbacks and hardships, perhaps even deliberate obstruction and ridicule. As we do, as we overcome, and conquer all that threatens our faith and love and our desire to serve, so an authority builds up within ourselves — spiritual authority.

This spills out into the community around, and, in ways often unknown to us, serves that community. Such authority is not our own, but comes from Christ. He met and overcame all manner of setbacks and humiliation and opposition, and he too received authority from God in his earthly life. It is this divine gift that he longs for us to accept from him.

Windbreak and Shade

**"I am the pine tree that shelters you; to me you
owe your fruit"**
(Hosea 14.8 NEB)

It is natural to be proud of one's achievements, yet all too easy to
be boastful and therefore a bore. Thinking of the image that was
given to Hosea in this Saying, I suppose a fruit tree or a shrub
could be proud of having borne its fruit. The fact is that it would
not have done so under the difficult weather conditions in
Palestine if it had not been protected from the stormy winds and
the summer sun by the nearby evergreens planted there for that
purpose.

We may consider those adversities that come upon us as
external forces interfering with our lives. Or it may be that
interior states of consciousness and emotion affect our lives even
more profoundly than the outside pressures from the world. It is
often far easier to escape from difficult material and social
circumstances coming from without, than it is from the searing
heat or whirlwinds of anger, jealousy, impatience, guilt, or from
our black clouds of depression and self-pity. How easy it is to
slide into these states when we really long to lead good, true and
beautiful lives.

Hosea knew a good deal about this in the turmoil of his own
life. He hears reassuring words from God which we can read in
the same chapter: "I will heal their backsliding, I will love them
freely"(verse 4). However much we slip back, the love of God
embraces us and nothing can take us outside that embrace,
because it is infinite. We often become anxious about the outcome
of our plans and activities because we are relying solely on
ourselves. When our efforts are guided by the Holy Spirit of God,

then his divine energy will accomplish God's will through us, and we can become willing instruments of the divine purpose. All the fruit comes from God, nothing from our own unaided efforts.

Understand that, you are really taking advantage of God's protection and shelter as well as his forgiveness. You will then grow in the best possible conditions and bring forth good fruit. The spirit and life of the Word of God, regularly heard and deeply received, will guarantee a bountiful harvest in the fullness of time as well as in God's eternity.

Wonderful Counsellor

"MY people ... I AM understanding"
(Isaiah 40-55 and Proverbs 8.14 AV)

Wisdom is one of the key attributes of the Divine. This is recognised widely in the biblical writings and in the contemporary thinking of other nations, notably ancient Egypt with its concept of *Maat*. The AV translation does justice to the link between Divine Wisdom and the beautiful human gift of empathy — feeling with and giving support to a fellow human, almost literally 'under-standing' or 'standing under' them in times of need or distress. This is more important than any other kind of aid, help, or counselling that may be on offer.

There is a lovely story that illustrates this. A mother asks her son: "What is the most important part of the body?" After a moment's thought he replies: "Ears." But his mother points out that, in spite of their handicap, deaf people manage very well. Some weeks later she repeats the question. Having had time to think it over, the boy says: "I know; eyes are the most important." Once again his mother asks him to think again, because blind people somehow cope with their disability remarkably well.

Months pass by, and the boy's grandfather dies. Everyone is sad and some are weeping. In the midst of the sorrow, the boy is astounded when his mother poses the question once again: "What is the most important part of the body?" The boy is confused and cannot reply; he just shakes his head. His mother says: "This is the time when you can begin to understand that your shoulders are the most important part of your body. Sooner or later, everyone needs a shoulder to cry on. My prayer for you is that you will always have some loving friend or relative who will provide you with a shoulder to cry on when you need it, and that you will always be ready to let others cry on your shoulder when others are similarly in need."

A minister was once asked for advice about pastoral counselling. He said: "Whenever I find myself in a counselling situation, I try to set up a three-way process of communication — self, client, God. Before we start, I recall this month's Saying, and as I listen, I try to be mindful of it, and of the Lord God who knows us better than we know ourselves, pouring out his loving wisdom."

You are Invited

"Come to ME, and listen to MY words; hear ME, and you shall have life"
(Isaiah 55.3 REB)

This Saying seems to lie behind the Divine Invitation given to us in St Matthew's Gospel [11.28]: "Come to me, all who are weary and whose load is heavy; I will give you rest."

Like children, we become absorbed in our own affairs; the busy, fleeting, often quarrelsome little world we create for ourselves fills our time and demands our full attention. Again, like children, we tend to turn a deaf ear when someone calls us away from our own concerns. For the happy child, the playground is preferable to the classroom. For adults too, there is greater attraction in the self-centred world than in life's true and often painful reality centred on the challenge of doing the will of God. Like children, we need to be called to order, back to the classroom, and be told to sit still and pay attention. And, yes, it is often very irksome when there seem to be other matters that need seeing to.

The voice of our all-loving Parent-Teacher is insistent. He calls us to higher things: "Come: come up here, and I will show you what must take place hereafter" (Revelation 4.1). The same voice calls Lazarus from his tomb: "Lazarus, come out" (John 11.43). I imagine God interpreting this to me: "Come out, come away from everything that leads to death. Listen to MY words. Escape from those constricting grave-clothes of purely human concerns, so many of which cause you anxiety. Stop your ceaseless and futile chatter. Listen to ME. My words are spirit and life."

How interesting it is that the Church has for centuries used Psalm 95 at the start of its daily morning prayer, the first two words of which are "O come … "

It is always helpful to listen for a couple of minutes to this divine invitation, or that from Matthew 11.28, to "Come" before you engage in contemplative prayer. Or sometimes, for a change, replace it with the words from Psalm 46.10: "Be still, and know that I AM God." Like the school's playground bell, it calls us to order and stillness before we get on with the work of listening to the Word of the Supreme Teacher.

Postscript

I take it that you have now tried this method of praying contemplatively, more or less in the manner I suggested in "Start Now" on pages five to nine. It is very likely that you are valuing more and more the time of stillness and quiet. Perhaps you have increased it from the original ten or fifteen minutes; or, if not, then you may be mildly annoyed that you cannot spend more time. If this is so, then it is time to begin the journey of exploration.

Let us assume for a moment that you are able to spend more time listening to the Word of God in this way. To begin with, before you start your quiet time, you could look up the Saying in the Bible and see the context in which it was originally spoken. You could also check out any other Bible references there may be in the commentary and mull over those for a moment.

Then, at the start of your prayer-time, as you relax and try to set aside the concerns and perhaps anxieties of the day, repeat mentally this Saying of Jesus recorded in Matthew 11.28, "Come to me, all you who labour and are heavy laden, and I will give you rest." This is one of many divine invitations given in the Bible which ask us to draw more closely to God and to off-load any cares or burdens that we may be carrying. Don't spend more than two minutes on this; then continue with the mental repetition of the Saying that you have chosen from the book. If distractions intrude, as they inevitably will, pay as little attention as possible to them, and edge them aside by re-focussing on the Saying.

You may then begin to experience the Word being spoken to you, rather than yourself mentally repeating it. It will first fill your mind, then it will penetrate more deeply within you as the silence deepens. By tradition we say that it begins to fill your heart — that little-known deeper layer of the inner self, beyond conscious thought and beneath our surface feelings and emotions. This won't happen in the first ten minutes of silence, but may begin after 15 to 20 minutes.

After reaching this level of contemplative prayer, say after 25 to 30 minutes, and before you thank God for the gift of his Word, you should bring into the silence some particular concern, or person, or group of people, for whom you wish to pray. You will probably have some individual or people in mind before you begin your contemplative prayer-time. If so, they may be put aside for 20 to 30 minutes while you hear God's Word and receive it into your mind and heart.

Then, towards the end of your time (which will by now probably have extended beyond 30 minutes) you can recall these intercession subjects. But instead of asking God to bless them, you will be speaking God's Word to them. That is to say, while you have them in mind, you focus again on the Saying, understanding that God is speaking his Word to them as well as to you:

"You, John . . . You, Mary . . . You, victims of violence . . . *Fear not; I am with you always.*"

In this fashion, you yourself are standing aside for a moment, with your feelings of concern, and allowing God's Word to work in the situation in all its divine Love, Wisdom and Power. You are acting as a reflector of the light of God's Word so that it may shine into a dark place; or as a channel of God's love so that it may flow more readily to those in need. This is contemplative intercession, and to engage in it is effectively to be doing the work of God in the world.

When you have spent five to ten minutes (perhaps longer) interceding in this way, then give thanks to God for his Word and offer yourself in his service. A complete prayer-exercise of this kind should not last less than about 40 minutes, and normally need last no longer than one hour.

* * *

I hope that I am right in thinking that you will have tried this way in prayer for a few weeks and that you want to continue. Experience shows that it is very difficult to carry on by yourself. So I want to leave you with just three pieces of advice which I hope you will be able to follow up.

Write to this address and ask for a free copy of the Introductory CD and other free literature:

FCP Administrator
117 Leicester Road Barnet
Herts
EN5 5EA
(address correct at time of going to press)

You may also like to visit this website:
www.contemplative-prayer.org.uk

If you can find one or two kindred spirits among your family, friends or acquaintances, share this way of praying with them on occasions.

Purchase a copy of the book *Exploring Contemplative Prayer* which I wrote with my fellow-author Peter Dodson. Our intention was to explain in a simple and straightforward way both the theory and practice of contemplative prayer. This is what Joyce Hugget wrote about the book:

I count it a privilege to recommend this book to anyone who is experiencing within themselves a hunger to pray contemplatively . . . so much more than a book, it is a companion on the most important journey any of us will ever make — the journey deeper into God.

The book was published in 2005 by Kevin Mayhew Ltd. at £7.99 and carries the ISBN number1 84417 494 8.

Sayings and commentaries that may be suitable for particular seasons and special days during the Church's Year:

Kingdom	18, 72, 108, 176, 178, 182
Advent	40, 102, 104, 114, 174
Christmas	34, 48, 80, 194
Epiphany	130, 156
Lent	46, 62, 96, 102, 104, ?, 114, 148
Holy Week and Easter	116, 128, 130, 166, 190, 196
Ascension	64, 124, 182, 186
Pentecost	44, 46, 160, 162
Trinity Sunday	30, 44, 80
Corpus Christi	12, 14
Transfiguration	50, 72, 124
New Year	10, 52, 130, 142, 152, 164

Bible References (page numbers in brackets)

Old Testament

Genesis

1	Night and Day (132)
1.31	Good for you (84)
15.1	Shield and Reward (158)
17.1	The Best (172)
22.22	True Love (188)

Exodus

3	Good Lord (86)
	Burning Question (46)
	Best Possession (34)
	Good Lord (86)
3.14-15	Safe with God (152)
	God's True Name (90)
4.12	Open thou our lips (136)
13.21	Burning Question (46)
14.13	Doing Nowt (56)
19.5-6	The Greatest (176)
	God's Choice (76)
24.12	Mountain Climbing (124)
32.20	Ethical Energy (62)
33.18	Good For You (84)

Leviticus

2.13	Salt of the Earth (154)
19.2	Holy God (100)
23.28	Doing Nowt (56)
26.12	Best Possession (34)

Numbers
12.3   Ethical Energy (62)

Deuteronomy
6.4   Night and Day (132)
10.14-15   God's Choice (76)
                             The Greatest (176)
16.11   True Vine (190)

Judges
6.14   Angels of the Lord (22)

1 Samuel
3.4   Angels of the Lord (22)
16.7   All Change (16)
                             Inside Out (102)
16.11   Angels of the Lord (22)

2 Samuel
6.17   Mobile God (120)
7.6   Mobile God (120)

1 Kings
3.14   My True Beginning (126)
19.9 & 13   Big Question (36)

2 Kings
20.6   Good Lord (96)

Psalms
12.6   God-Space (82)
                             Molten Metal (122)

Joel
1.15   Success Story (168)

Micah
6.8   Holy God (100)

Haggai
1.5   Lifestyle (114)
2.5   Breath of God (44)

Zechariah
13.9   Molten Metal (122)

Malachi
3.1-3   Molten Metal (122)
3.2-3   Bang Bang (26)
                        Burning Question (46)
3.6-7   Pole Star (144)

Apocrypha

Ecclesiasticus
24.18   God the Mother (74)
                        [NRSV margin]

Baruch
4.30   Known by Name (110)

2 Esdras
16.73   Molten Metal (122)

BOOKS

O is a symbol of the world, of oneness and unity. In different cultures it also means the "eye," symbolizing knowledge and insight. We aim to publish books that are accessible, constructive and that challenge accepted opinion, both that of academia and the "moral majority."

Our books are available in all good English language bookstores worldwide. If you don't see the book on the shelves ask the bookstore to order it for you, quoting the ISBN number and title. Alternatively you can order online (all major online retail sites carry our titles) or contact the distributor in the relevant country, listed on the copyright page.

See our website **www.o-books.net** for a full list of over 500 titles, growing by 100 a year.

And tune in to myspiritradio.com for our book review radio show, hosted by June-Elleni Laine, where you can listen to the authors discussing their books.

MySpiritRadio